CROSSING OCEANS, SAVING LIVES: A DOCTOR'S JOURNEY

By Dattatreyudu Nori, M.D.

Chapter 1
PRELUDE

On January 25, 2015, my phone rang. It was the Indian Consulate in New York. Three days earlier, I had attended a dinner in recognition of my accomplishments at the home of Mr. Varindeer Bhalla, President of the Indian American Forum. There I had met Mr. Sri Jananeswar Moolay, who at that time was the Consul General of India to the U.S. and a poet and a writer. Mr. Moolay is passionate about education and service. I was surprised three days later to get a phone call from him. He was calling to congratulate me on the Indian government's decision to confer "Padmashri" on me. After the dinner, Mr. Moolay had received the news of the decision, but the government had not provided my contact number. However, Mr. Moolay contacted Mr. Bhalla, obtained my phone number from him, and officially communicated the news to me. He also provided a release to the press and other media. After that, my phone refused to stop ringing.

PADMA AWARD

Every year, on the night of January 25, The Indian Union government announces Padma awards to the award recipients and on January 26, the Republic Day of India, their names are announced to the press.

The actual award ceremony is scheduled on two dates, one in the ensuing March and the other in April. I selected the date in April to make travel arrangements for myself and my family (my wife, son, and daughter).

A senior IAS (Indian Administrative Service) officer was assigned to us for the communications regarding the program. All of us landed in New Delhi on April 4, 2015, where we were received by a liaison officer from the Home Ministry.

The accommodation provided was at the Taj Hotel. We stayed there only for a few hours, however, as we were asked by Mr. K.P. Singh* (more about him a little later) to move to his own Hotel Aman.

We collected all the necessary program information, rehearsal time, etc., and moved to Hotel Aman. I reviewed the rehearsal and the actual ceremony particulars and was extremely impressed with the minute- by-minute details. After a few hours of rest, all of us were taken to the "Rashtrapathi Bhavan," the venue for the rehearsal as well as for the actual award ceremony the next day.

I was thrilled and amazed at the spectacular decoration and the meticulous planning, even for the rehearsal. I was provided with the protocol information on exactly where to sit, the chair number, the walking route, and the distance from my location to the podium where the president would be, as well as how to greet the president and even to which side I'd have to look to get the official photo op with the president.

On the day of the award ceremony, we were seated as planned while my family was sitting in the guest arena.

I cannot describe in words my boundless excitement or how I felt at that moment to be there receiving the award.

It was not only a prestigious recognition by my motherland for my contribution in the field of medicine but also unique as I was one of the two or three NRI (Non Resident Indian) physicians out of 30,000 in the US to receive this award since its introduction in 1954.

Receiving Padmashri award from
His excellency the President of India Mr. Pranab Mukherjee

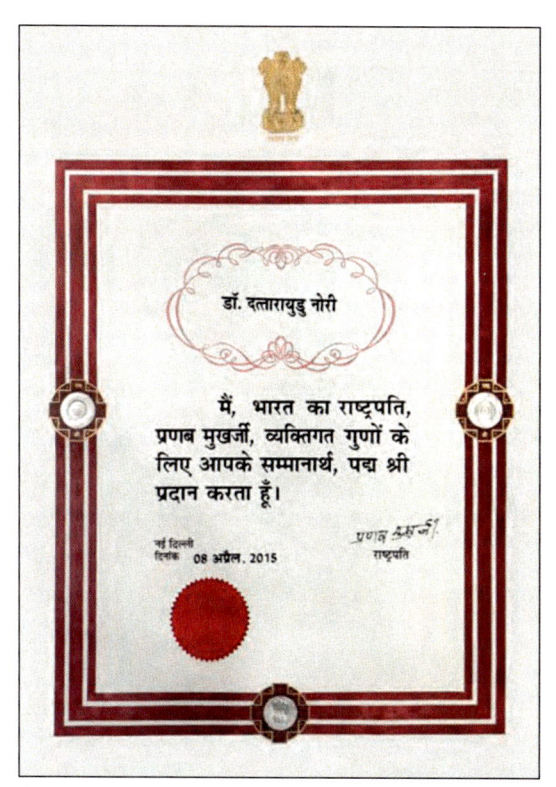

Picture of Padma Award Signed by the President

Suddenly, I remembered my mother: her love for me, the hardships she had undergone to bring me up and to provide my education, her continuous encouragement to make me strive to accomplish…. If only my mother could have been alive…. how happy she would have been! The very thought caused tears to well up in my eyes. Yet while silently paying my homage to her, I controlled my emotions.

Slowly the VIP hall was filled with all the dignitaries, including the Hon. Prime Minister of India, Mr. Narendra Damodardas Modi, all the cabinet ministers and ambassadors, top government officials, and invited guests of the government.

If I have to describe it in one phrase, it represented "the Power House of India" all in one place.

One of the ceremony planners, a senior IAS officer, who happens to be from my state, Andhra Pradesh of Federal India, helped my family to get the best seats in the guest arena and also asked them to stand up and applaud when I received the award from the president, even though that is against the protocol. They did exactly as instructed by him and were seen in all the media coverage of the event all across India!

I received my award from the then president of India, Mr. Pranab Mukherjee. After the award ceremony the president gave a reception for all of the award recipients, which was attended by all the members of this powerhouse. During the reception, our US Ambassador to India, Mr. Richard Verma, approached me and congratulated me as I was the only US citizen receiving this prestigious award.

Then a group photo was arranged with the President, the Vice President, the Prime Minister, the Home Minister, and other cabinet ministers and award recipients.

After staying for a couple of days in Delhi, we went to Hyderabad and other towns as the festivities were continued by various organizations in Hyderabad, Vijayawada, and Guntur, etc.

Back to my Padma award...

When I received the Padma Award, I was overwhelmed with joy and pride. India, my beloved homeland has recognized my accomplishments in the field of oncology and had chosen me out of many other highly qualified candidates. My commitment and dedication to my specialty has led to the position as the Chief at Memorial Sloan-Kettering Cancer Research Institute in Manhattan, New York, which is considered as the premier cancer research institute in the world. I thought about all the events in my life that contributed to this recognition, and many others such as "Tribute to Life Award from the American Cancer Society", one of the highest civilian awards in the U.S. "Ellis Island Medal of Honor", "Living Legend in Oncology Award from Indian Oncology Congress", and "Top Doctors for Cancer in the U.S. for three decades".

I was born in the remote village of Mantada in the state of Andhra Pradesh, India. My father died when I was 6 years old. I was raised by my mother who provided me unconditional love and support. Due to her sacrifices, I am what I am today... Above all I am thankful to the almighty God for showering his blessings on me and to all my teachers, mentors, and especially my patients who inspired and helped me throughout my personal and professional journey.

I am writing this book to express my gratitude and happiness to everyone.

With our honorable Prime Minister Narendra Modi during his visit to New York

Chapter 2

PROLOGUE

To write or not to write is a Hamlet's dilemma. Penning one's own life story is much more so. "Writing a book is a horrible, exhausting struggle...." Says George Orwell, but he adds in the same breath that this urge cannot be resisted. My case is no exception. I am inspired by the stories of eminent people and by my encounters with some of them. Whenever an autobiography is written, it is not necessarily written only to highlight or to boast about one's own accomplishments, but to leave a trail of tribulation and triumph, the saga of struggle and success for contemporaries and posterity to glean and to gain from it whatever is beneficial to their own progress in life, to shut out and shun whatever is detrimental, and to build character and a life, brick by brick. "Don't forget: No one sees the world the way you do, so no one can tell the stories that you have to tell" (Charles de Lint). Each one has a story! Presenting that story is an endeavor to repay the debt due to society. To recollect all those who have showered their love on you. To recall the arduous path you tread unwaveringly. To celebrate the journey. In brief, to touch every part of the past enthralling you. To be conscious that you have been an infinitesimal but valuable part of the unending annals of the progression of human life and civilization. To immerse in that overwhelming joy once again!

Although I hailed from a very poor family with a humble background, I was fortunate to become one of the most world-renowned cancer specialists. If my story can inspire one individual or many to contribute to the science of medicine, my objective is accomplished. I hope some may emulate my life.

I am a strong believer in the circle of life. My definition of the circle of life consists of 1. My family, 2. My community, 3. My country of origin, 4. My country of settlement. The circle is concentric with me at its center.

After realizing that specifically, I have started writing my autobiography. Primarily, I would like to share these four topics with one and all.

It is often said that a person comes into the world alone and exits alone. But that was not true in my case in the sense that there were eleven siblings before I was born. They were all eager to love me, and I have always had a huge family to nurture me. It is important that I state this because had it not been for my dear brothers' role in my upbringing and education, perhaps I would have not been whatever I am today. The affection and the warmth my family share and that binds us I would like once more to fondly recall through this book.

Whether it is because of globalization or otherwise, if once they settle down in a good job or calling, the present generation often keeps a kind of superficial relationship with parents, siblings, relatives, and others. For generations to come, some may never know the bond that prevails in a closely integrated, large family. Perhaps my affinity with my brothers and sisters may be a guiding element for presenting the concept of such a bond here. It is the primary intention for documenting my family experiences in this book.

As a professional doctor, the research I have done is of immense importance. Rendering ultra-modern treatment in a well-equipped country, such as the U.S., with all the appropriate infrastructure is one thing, but the daunting task of delivering a similar service to the common man in India is another. The massive effort I have put forward in that direction has been a crucial endeavor. To disseminate the result to everybody is my second intention. To share the conviction and the unrelenting hard work involved in establishing The Basava Tarakam Indo-American Cancer Institute in Hyderabad, India, and recollecting and acknowledging the generous help of many people towards that objective is another primary motive to write this book.

Many fear cancer. If detected in the early stages and treated suitably, it is not impossible to recover from cancer. Many times, doctors and their patients encounter cancer and emerge successful; this inspires others too. Those who are newly diagnosed with cancer gather hope and courage to fight against it. Therefore, such inspiring stories of my patients I have shared in this book.

Apart from that, I have also documented the latest developments that are taking place in the treatment of cancer. Earlier, surgery and removal of the affected part was thought to be the only way to treat this disease. Because of that, even if cancer were cured, patients would suffer from the loss of some part of their body. More recently, radiation has brought significant improvements in the treatment regime. To help people become aware of the developments, I have tried to broadly outline both the current research and research that has taken place in the recent past. The innovative trials that are taking place in targeted therapy, genome therapy, precision medicine, immuno-therapy, stereotactic radiation, a combination of the latter two, next generation sequencing (NGS,) and the molecular twin concept give further hope for the future.

The treacherous path I have tread to reach this stage in my life and career was strewn with many impediments, setbacks, and challenges. When I look back, I wonder whether it was I who crossed all these barriers.

For the sake of a unified presentation, I have divided this book into several sections juxtaposed against one another, although life runs in a continuum in several channels.

Let me start from my modest moorings.

The beginning….

One's roots define one's growth. The world may see one's achievements, but only that "one" knows how strongly he has been supported for such progress. My simple religious origins, the culture, my motherland, and the country that gave me shelter, succor and success, the students that adored me, the blessings that abounded from my dear patients, my "Gurus" who held my hand and guided me to the right path, and the omnipotent, omnipresent Almighty without whose benevolence I could have not been what I am today -- To cherish all of that and to relive all those significant moments, I am sharing my eventful story.

My parents
Nori Satya Narayana and Nori Kanaka Durgamba.

Chapter 3

MY CHILDHOOD AND FAMILY

After over 200 years of servitude under colonialism, India gained independence on Aug 15, 1947. Within 2 months thereafter on Oct 21, 1947, I was born.

Nori Satyanarayana was my father. My mother's name was Nori Kanaka Durgamba. While my father was named after a Hindu God, my mother was named after a Hindu Goddess.

My father was a teacher in a government school. He was transferred every 2 or 3 years. I vaguely remember the days when he was serving in a village by the name of Tadanki in the combined Madras province of Young India.

I was born in a village called Mantada, near Vuyyuru in the Krishna district of the then Madras presidency. Now, it is in the Pamidimukkala sub-division of Nuziveedu revenue division of the present state of Andhra Pradesh (In the Federal Republic of India, there are over 30 states. Gurajada, Garikaparru, Kapileswara Puram, and Yakamooru were some of the hamlets near my village, while Vuyyuru, Kalavapamula, Pamarru, Pedaparupudi, Thotavallooru were bigger villages nearby.) My home was in a village called Thotavallooru. My childhood, as I recollect, I spent in that village.

The nearest city was Vijayawada, which was 35 kilometers away.

My father was spiritual in nature. Every Sunday he used to observe the vow of silence, his shoulders always adorned with a saffron cloth. During the school holidays and in the evenings, he used to give discourses on the popular Hindu epics: "The Ramayana" (the story of Lord Rama, the Hindu God), "The Bhagavata" (the story of Lord Krishna, the Hindu God) and "Devi Bhagavatam" (the story of Devi Kali, the Hindu Goddess). My mother was also deeply religious and she always, as a matter of routine, used to recite "Lalita Sahasra Namam" (The thousand names of the Goddess Lalita).

There was a spiritual woman, named Picchamma, in the

nearby village of Kurumaddali. As long as she was alive, my parents used to devoutly serve her. Even after her death, they showed the same devotion by visiting her "samadhi" (tomb). Near Mantada, where I was born, there was an "ashram" (hermitage) in the adjacent Kurumaddali village. During the popular Hindu festival of "Navaratri," also known

as "Dasara," food used to be distributed to the needy all through that period by the hermitage. To contribute to that social cause, my father donated half of his ancestral agricultural land (one acre out of his total 2 acre property) in favor of the hermitage.

My parents had 12 children: six girls and six boys. I was the youngest. It was 1954. I was six years old.

That year in "Chaitra," the first month of the Hindu calendar, on the auspicious occasion of "Sri Ramanavami" (the festival celebrating the birth and wedding of Lord Sri Rama, the Hindu God), arrangements were being made for the commemoration of Lord Sri Rama's wedding in the village of Kurumaddali. My father set out to attend the event. He was to catch a bus from Thotavallooru village. I can vividly recall the way I ran behind him, hoping to accompany him to Kurumaddali village. When the bus arrived, it was already crowded to overflowing. My father managed to find a spot for himself on the steps of the footboard of the bus.

But I didn't relent. I ran behind the bus. Seeing me, my father got the bus to stop, alighted, and as a gesture of affection, gave me two Anna coins (coinage during those days corresponding roughly to 1/900 of a U.S. dollar) to buy some treats for myself. He assured me that he would return home by that night.

But I never surmised that he would fail in his promise. Yes, he broke his promise. Rather, it was destined that way.

Later, I was told that my father had gone into a huge canal of the River Krishna for a religious ablution and was swept away by the sudden flow of swirling waters as the sluice gates were opened at Balliparru village up above the stream without giving any warning to the public.

As we did not have any inkling of any of these things, all of us were happily celebrating the festival at our village, Thotavallooru, wearing new clothes as is the tradition.

My maternal uncle Mr. Annambhatla Subbarao used to live with us in Thotavallooru village. He was the postmaster, and his house was the post office.

A postal messenger shouted "telegram" from outside our door. In those days a telegram invariably meant bad news.

As was expected of a telegram, it revealed that my father was missing in the Krishna waters. Everybody at home broke down with sorrow.

But somewhere a flickering hope was fluttering in our hearts, expecting some miracle – somehow that God would rescue him and my father would return home. All of us waited with bated breath throughout the night.

While tears were rolling down my cheeks, I was reportedly praying to God: "No, my father must not be swept away by the Krishna waters. He must come back, hale and healthy."

Initially, I was sitting in front of the God's picture praying to him while the holy "diyas" were burning, but then I got into a fit of rage and shouted at the God, started quarrelling with him, threatening him, "Send my father back home! Send him! Otherwise, I will not keep quiet…" . My sisters later told me that I had fought with the God like that for a long time.

my sisters left to right Smt. Pillalamari Padmavati, Smt. NimmagaddaAnantha Lakshmi, Smt. Meduri Seethamahalakshmi, Smt. Lanka Indira Devi and Smt. Lanka Rama Devi.

Alas! Our prayers were not favorably answered. The next day, my father's dead body was found at the sluice gates of Gudlavalleru village. It was brought home. Everybody was weeping. I wept inconsolably. Although I could not understand then the magnitude of losing one's father, what I could understand better was that I would not have his love anymore.

The son of my maternal uncle apparently asked me,
"Hey Dattu!
What would you do if you found a glass broken?"

I promptly answered, of course, quite innocently,

"What would I
do?! I would throw it away."

Taking the cue from my response, my uncle's son continued, "If once life is lost, the body is like that broken glass. Your father's life is lost. But his soul will remain with us. Then, why should we weep over the lifeless body?"

I do not know how much and what I had understood of his comments. But, after my brother-in-law pacified me in that way, I never ever wept again about my father's death. My sisters wonder about it even today. When I contemplate the situation, I feel that perhaps my father had seeded his spiritual traits in me.

* an oil lamp usually made from clay, with a cotton wick dipped in ghee or vegetable oils. Diyas, native to the Indian subcontinent, are often used in Hindu, Sikh, Jain and Zoroastrian religious festivals such as Diwali or Khushti ceremonies.

My father was 54 when he died.

He had known astrology thoroughly. We later found a notebook where he had written down predictions regarding his own life. He had noted the planetary congruence and its impact on his life, etc. But, about 1954, he had marked the date with a circle in red and left it empty. He had not written anything thereafter!

My father's unexpected death left us in turmoil.

My father's job and his one acre of arable land could only sustain my family hand to mouth. The education of all the sons and the marriages of some of the daughters were still unaccomplished, or due. We had lost our entire source of support. But how my mother managed the family, how she dealt with all the problems without ever making any difficulty public was commendable. I feel proud to recollect that it was solely her courage and undaunted will that helped us to become self-reliant and settle down in life thereafter. At the same time, I also feel pained to reflect about her then endless difficulties.

My elder sisters Padmavati, Ananata Lakshmi, Seeta Mahalakshmi, and Maha Tripura Sundari were married. My eldest brother, Radhakrishna Moorthy, was born after those four sisters. He was working an economics lecturer in a Machilipatnam college when my father passed away. My second and third brothers, Mrityunjaya Rao and Ramamohan Rao, were studying in different colleges in the state.

So, only my other two brothers, Madhura Babu and Rama Theerdha, and two elder sisters, Indira Devi and Ramadevi, apart from me, the last of the siblings, remained with my mother at Thotavallooru village. I shudder and my tears well up to recollect how my mother managed all the difficulties without others coming to know of them.

I remember very well how my mother never used to use the harvest of the paddy, but pounded it into small grains of rice and sold it to the neighbors. I also recollect how she was constrained to sell her two gold bangles to pay my brother's college fee. The list doesn't end there. Those were very painful days. Even today, I shudder with sorrow to recall them.

And that had a deep impact on me.

During those days, there was nobody to help my mother. Sisters of my father could be of help in some sundry work, but they were also not financially sound. Their home, which housed the post office that delivered the news of my father's death by a telegram, used to always scare us. My maternal uncle who was handling the minor job of postmaster also died young with some unknown fever (pyrexia of unknown origin).

During those difficult times, my aunty, the elder sister of my mother, Jonnalagadda (Telugu-speaking people invariably carry initials of their clan, this is one case) Sundaramma stood by mother like a rock. She became a widow at a young age and had a daughter. Although they were not very rich, they had some agricultural lands in the village of Chinna Mutthevi village and had a relatively better income when compared to that of our family. She funded our education. She was of a helping nature and spiritual. Neighbors called her a "Philosopher." Every evening many people used to assemble to listen to her discourses.

Each one of my elder brothers gradually went for higher studies and secured good jobs. Thereafter, extending their helping hand for a few years to the sibling next in line in that endeavor was more like a routine ritual. All of us brothers, therefore, were able to obtain good positions, and all my elder sisters were married into respectable families.

Although my family was not financially sound, there has never been any dearth of love and affection among us. As I was the last of the children and lost my father at a very young age, not only my mother, but everybody, used to pamper me a lot. They always used to keep a few special sweets and treats especially for me. Also, they used to spare the yogurt for me while they used to settle for buttermilk for their meals.

In our village Thotavallooru, we had two old temples. One was dedicated to Lord Sri Venugopala Swamy and his consorts, Rukmini and Satyabhama. The second was dedicated to Lord Sri Chenna Mallikarjuna Swamy and his consort, Bhramarambha. I can fondly recall the temples because for children like us, after every special "pooja" (worship), they used to liberally distribute the "prasadam" (part of the holy offering of food to the deities) of "pulihora" and "guggillu" (both popular food items from South India). I used to especially like the "chitti gare" (a sweet cookie) that was given in the Shivite temple of Lord Sri Mallikarjuna. As children, we used to crave these treats and patiently wait for them until the "prasadam" was distributed.

Chapter 4
EDUCATION AND PROFESSION DREAMS AND DIFFICULTIES

I could not recollect whether my father had admitted me to any school. But, for certain, I remember that before his leaving for his school, my father used to teach me some poetry and "shlokas" (religious chants in Sanskrit) and I was to learn them by rote and recite to him in the evening when he returned.

I don't remember anything about my primary education. Although there was a school in Thotavallooru village, I don't recollect anything about my father admitting me to the school or anything like that. It was the only school for 3 or 4 nearby villages.

I can remember that because an uncle of mine used to live in the nearby Bhadraji Palem. His son used to come to Thotavallooru by bicycle to attend the school. Before going to the school, he would come to my house, leave his meal box at my home and go to school. I used to open the carrier and stealthily taste all the dishes and repack the carrier. Sometimes when my "tasting spree" became excessive, his meal box used to go empty, but he never admonished me, nor complained to my mother.

As mentioned above, at the time of my father's death, my eldest brother was already married and working as an economics lecturer in National College, Machilipatnam. Among my elder brothers, one was attending graduate school, another post-graduate. After my father's death, we continued to live in Thotavallooru for 1 or 2 more years. As both of my brothers were pursuing higher studies, my mother decided to shift to my eldest brother's home at Machilipatnam. My brothers concurred with that decision.

My elder sister Indira often tells me that I had my early education in the nearby school of Potta Picchaiah. Although I don't remember that, I vividly remember Indira's marriage. Her in-laws home was also very close by. My brother-in-law and his mother used to like me and pamper me a lot as I was a very young child. But I always used to accuse them of stealing my sister and plead with them to send her back to my house. Of course, my sister's mother-in-law used to laugh it away. My sister would pacify me, give me some snacks, and then drop me home. Similarly, I used to visit my eldest and second sisters at Vijayawada and Eluru respectively and spend time with them. While I was in Eluru, we received a telegram. We were afraid.

The telegram read, "Send Dattu to Bunder immediately." (To the port; Bunder was another name for Machilipatnam as it had a port of active trade.)

To our relief, it was not any bad news as we had feared. One of my distant uncles, Nori Narasimham, was a teacher in the J branch government school. To get admission into that school, prospective students were to undergo a test and an interview. My uncle not only assured my brothers of my admission but somehow completed the ritual of the test by posing several questions to me and finally obtained my admission there!

For a year or two, I studied at this school. By that time, my third brother Rammohanrao got married and began a job in Kurnool. To reduce the burden on my elder brother, my mother shifted to Kurnool along with me and my two sisters. I joined my 3rd standard in the B Camp School there.

It must be between 1960 and 1962 as I remember that Sri Damodaram Sanjeevaiah, the chief minister of then combined Andhra Pradesh state, had come to Kurnool and laid the foundation stone for the construction of the permanent structures for the school. I used to play on the sand and the construction site of the foundation.

In 1953, when a linguistic state of Andhra Pradesh was carved out for Telugu- speaking people from the former combined Madras province, Kurnool was the capital of the state for the first three years. Kurnool was divided, for administrative convenience, as A, B, C camps, and the government offices and the quarters of their employees were also accommodated there according to the official hierarchy. My brother was allocated quarters in C camp.

The only friend from Kurnool I remember is Saikumar. His father's post was one cadre above my brother's, and I think they were staying in D camp. The headmaster of my school used to conduct "tuition" (a kind of coaching apart from what is being taught at the school), and also, he used to give away the question papers to those students who attended his tuition session on the eve of the exam. I could not attend his tuition as we were not financially sound. But Saikumar used to call me in the night to the backyard of his house and share all the questions.

The darkness of the night, the anxiety to know the questions, making a trip to his place without others knowing it, writing down the maximum number of questions on my palm in an instant all used to create a weird feeling in me at that young age.

After my completing my 3rd, 4th and 5th standards at Kurnool, my second brother, Mrityunjaya Rao, took us to his place at Guntur, another big town near Vijayawada. I studied for two years in Majeti Guravayya high school. There used to be a teacher named Narasayya who was a role model with his impeccable conduct and excellent teaching skills that inspired many a student.

In the meanwhile, my eldest brother Radha Krishnamoorthy was selected for the Indian Police service (I.P.S.). Hence, he resigned his post at the National College, Machilipatnam. But, in a strange coincidence, my 4th brother Madhura Babu joined that vacancy the next day! So, we shifted to Machilipatnam again.

For a long time, the students of the National College used to remark with amazement over an anecdote about the students of the economics section who had burst into laughter when my 4th brother told them, "I will continue the lesson from where my elder brother has left off." I continued my education in Jai Hind High School in Machilipatnam.I did my S.S.L.C. (school final) there. After that I entered my P.U.C., i.e. pre-university course (pre graduation) in National College there. My elder sister Ramadevi was one year senior to me. She studied Arts. College authorities use to collect both of our college fees in advance from my lecturer brother Madhura Babu's monthly salary, which was almost the entire sum!

What times were they? Even today, those pathetic days somehow ring fear in me...There was no cooking gas. Cooking was done by burning wood sticks or sawdust. I used to struggle to pedal a bicycle which was oversized for me to transport huge bags of sawdust for that purpose. I also used to bring coal bags

for the oven of coal embers. I was the

with my mother In Guntur during my elementary schooling.

errand boy to fetch whatever things were needed for the house from the corner store or a shop. The grocery store manager used to shout at me for asking for additional credit without paying the earlier charges due. I used to patiently endure this scolding and convince him to get what I wanted, then drag myself home with the bags. Not one or two, but many such incidents from the past make me feel heavy at heart even today! Nobody should undergo such a childhood.

My sister Ramadevi used to help my mother and sister-in-law in their domestic chores and hence came late to college.

During those tumultuous times, it was the love and affection that prevailed among our brothers and sisters that gave us some stability and kept us calm. Not that, in our large family, there were no routine, small differences of opinion, but the affection and love and the nature to help one another far surpassed such things and overshadowed them. Affection, love, and helping one another created an unbreakable bond among us. Even my brothers-in-law and sisters-in-law embraced the same attitude and remained in the same ambit of affection. That's why, even today, the equal connections with one another and the relationships among us are intact and flourishing.

It had been my big dream to become a doctor for a long time. I don't know why such a dream struck me at such a young age, but it started becoming very intense and never waned. In those days, the society used to look at doctors as demi-gods, if not gods. The glamour, the dignity, and the huge reputation of a doctor in the town were unparalleled, and no other profession, perhaps, commanded that. Another incident gave an impetus to this.

In Machilipatnam, there used to live nearby a doctor by the name Dr. Subbarao. He owned an Ambassador car (an Indian automobile brand, made by Hindustan motors heavily patronized by the govt. of independent India, it was a symbol of social status in those days). It was chauffeur driven. People used to show a lot of respect and greet the doctor when he was going around the town or going to the hospital. Seeing that, my resolve to become a doctor further gained momentum.

One day, in a sheer childish act, I tried to open the door of his parked car in front of his house. His driver saw that and hit me, using abusive

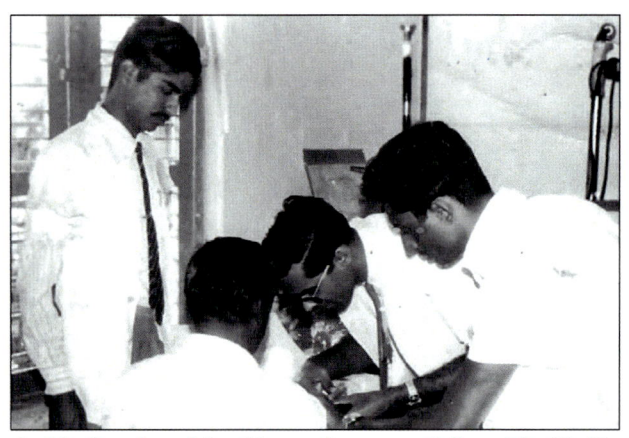

in the biochemistry lab with my classmates left to right. Dr Varada Reddy, and Dr Venkat Kumar at Kurnool Medical College.

language without minding my being a child. That made a very deep impact on my mind. That day I resolved, with a kind of vengeance, to study very hard, become a doctor and buy a bigger car than that.

In those days, there were no entrance exams – as we have today – to gain entry into any professional course, nor were ranks considered. However, if one scored very good marks in the pre-graduation course, P.U.C. (Pre-University Course), one could get admitted into medicine. Therefore, I focused on my P.U.C. with a great deal of sincere effort in order to get into medicine. But I was not admitted. Although I had a good score, I did not have the additional certificates of N.C.C. (National Cadet Corps) or N.S.S. (National Social Service). Yet, I took a stubborn stand at home with my family members about wanting to study medicine no matter how severe my difficulties were. My brothers and mother felt that I was not able to understand the difficulty in getting admission into medicine.

They gave me some 20 or 30 rupees (Indian currency) and said to me, "Go to Warangal Private Medical College, and find out the procedure and fee details for the course. They also gave me the address of a "choultry" (a public lodging facility in India) there. As I alighted in the Warangal railway station, I summoned a manual rikshaw puller and asked him urbanely to take me to that "choultry." He looked at me askance, surveyed me from top to toe and blurted out, "The building opposite to you is that choultry" and left. Then, I realized my innocence.

I visited the medical college at Warangal. The cost according to the prospectus of the course itself was 200 to 300 rupees, and the capitation fee and other fees would total to about 10,000 rupees, I was told. As my family members had tried to tell me, I now realized how medical education was far from my reach! Disappointed, I returned to Machilipatnam. But my desire to pursue medicine never left me I thought I would get my B.Sc. and try my luck again for admission into medicine thereafter. I was advised to do my B.Sc. in Agriculture. But it required a certificate from a local agriculture officer. I approached one for the certificate in a fertilizer shop in Machilipatnam and told him that I knew a bit about agriculture.

He asked me, "How long does it take to till an acre of agricultural land?"

"One month," I answered him immediately. He looked at me with surprise and then smiled.

"You said you knew about agriculture," he said and quickly

added, "It takes only a part of the day or a day to till one acre," and sent me home. Thus, my attempt to get into a B.Sc. Agriculture program also failed.

Those days, learning typing appeared to be an additional advantage in getting a job for the middle class of the society, so I was also advised to enroll in a typing institute. Although it would not have been anything difficult for me to learn typing and get into some job, I did not want to become a typist for life. I, therefore, did not enroll in any typing institute. After the summer holidays, I entered B.Sc. at National College.

I met and became friendly with one Samayam Ramarao, who later became a Circle Inspector of Police (Station House Officer). Another friend was Jaswanth Babu, who later joined Andhra Sugars, Ltd. A distant relative who became a friend was Kota Nagendra Prasad. He was also from a large family; his brothers were friends of my brothers. Whereas I did not have my father, his father was a important officer in a bank. But that did not come between us in becoming friends. People used to call us "Krishna and Arjun," the great pals from the great Indian Hindu epic, "Maha Bharat."

We used to study together. We had some fun and playfulness, too. Together, we would gather leaves and flowers for the festival of "Ganesh Chaturthi" (a Hindu festival devoted to Lord Ganesh, the God who addresses all impediments). Even for a festival mostly of women, "Atla Thadiya" (Atla Tadde)*, we used to create all hustle and bustle. Also, despite his father's great care, we used to eat most of the mangoes borne by the tree in their backyard. Also, during monsoon, some benches used to get drenched in the classroom. Fearing that classes might still be conducted despite this if other benches were available, we used to pour water on the rest of them and soak them to avoid classes.

All said, I never left my dream of pursuing medicine. Hence, after completing my B.Sc., I did apply for admission into medicine. Andhra University at Vizag was to take a final call sifting through all applicants. My brother, who was the superintendent of police in charge of Vijayanagaram district, took pains to personally visit Vizag and found out that I had gotten a seat at Kurnool Medical College.

Another 20 to 30 B.Sc. graduates, like me, were also admitted there.

*Atla Taddi is a traditional festival celebrated by married Hindu women of Andhra Pradesh for the health and long life of their husbands. It occurs on the 3rd night after the full moon in Aswiyuja month of Telugu calendar and falls in either September or October in the Gregorian calendar.[1] It is the Telugu equivalent of Karva Chauth, which is celebrated by North Indian women the following day. (courtesy, Wikipedia)

Dream comes true!

In June 1965, I joined medicine in Kurnool Medical College. I was happy that my long-time dream was coming true. But there was an initial hiccup in the process. As I mentioned, another 20 to 30 B.Sc. graduates were admitted to the same college. Of course, all of us got 1½ yrs. Of exemption. Also, if we were to pass one more exam in physics, almost two years of the course would be over. The concerned professor told us that we should stay there at Kurnool for the year without taking any classes while we waited to take the exam. We would not be allowed to enter the 2nd year in the medical college until then. At that point, none of us had any lodging and boarding facilities there. As guided by the professor, if we were to stay there for one year just to take one exam in physics, it would be a sizeable financial burden for all of us. We started deliberating thereupon. That was the first time that the leader in me surfaced.

We investigated the professor. He had 2 or 3 daughters of marriageable age, so he needed money. But he was not a corrupt man; nor were we corrupt. On behalf of the group, I represented our case to him.

I persuaded him, "Sir! None of us have money to stay here for even 30 days. That doesn't mean that we are against taking the exam, nor are we not unfamiliar with the subject of physics. Kindly allow us to come here one day before the exam. We will collect from among us half of the estimated cost of our room and board and pay you. Please don't insist upon our staying here for the entire year."

I don't know in what state of mind he was at that time, but he agreed to my proposition. All of us returned home and attended the exam as planned and scored good marks too. As promised, we also paid him. He was happy; so were we. Unlike most people think, I realized that without overstepping, we can obtain what we want. It was a win-win for both. That incident has further strengthened my conviction that to solve any problem, there is no need for any friction but, instead, a constructive dialogue can suffice.

In the application for the entrance into medical school, I had given my mother's address. Since she didn't have any income, accordingly, my fee was also relatively less. But the truth remained that even that amount was a huge burden to us. My aunt Jonnalagadda Sundaramma paid my tuition fee. Had I stayed in a dormitory, it would have been an additional burden. So, I shared a private accommodation, renting with another three friends. Sometimes, we used to cook at the tenement, sometimes we used to eat out. We maintained a monthly account in a hotel called Woodlands Hotel in Kurnool.

Kodanda Rami Reddy, Ramachandra Varma, and Palakurti Satyanarayana were my good friends, classmates, and roommates during my M.B.B.S. days in Kurnool. Kodanda Rami Reddy has been successfully practicing at Nellore town in Andhra Pradesh. Ramachandra Varma retired recently after his successful career as a medical doctor in Florida, in the U.S. Satyanarayana used to practice as a pediatrician at Bhimavaram in Andhra Pradesh; he is no more.

I have to share here some funny experiences I had with Satyanarayana. From Palakollu town of Andhra Pradesh, he was a Vysya by caste (trading caste; India has an age-old caste system broadly called "Chatur Varnashrama": Four echelons of society; each one's caste is decided by their calling in the hierarchy of Hindu society). If I requested a loan of Rs.15, he would give me Rs. 20. Initially, I thought he was generous. But, one day he told me that it was better to lend a round figure for easy calculation of accounts. Whenever I received some money from my aunt, I would repay him.

There were very poor phone facilities those days in the nascent republic of India; only rich people, some offices, and post offices had phones. For commoners, the mode of communication was through post cards and inland letters (both sold and purveyed by post offices run by the government). My aunty used to drop a post card communicating to me when she would likely send me the money by money order. The card also brought news of the well-being of everybody at home. Therefore, the post card that used to come from Machilipatnam was like my lifeline. Accordingly, I would carefully budget my expenses at Kurnool.

Once it so happened that my money order was delayed. Even the post card that preceded it also did not come. Every day I anxiously waited.

One fateful day, it became very cloudy and started raining. I rushed to my room from the college. But I could not help getting drenched. When I opened the door, there was a post card. Those days, the postmen used to push the letters underneath the closed doors. I was immensely happy to see the post card, but my happiness did not last even for a minute because all the writing had gotten drenched and washed away as it had been exposed to the rain. Those were the days of pen and ink, unlike the present where we use ballpoint pens. Seeing the ruined post card, I almost broke down.

During such tough times, Satyanarayana and other friends used to come to my rescue.

"It's ok, Dattu! You can return it after you receive the money order," was the usual refrain from my friends when they lent me the money and helped me. To have such friends was a boon!

By that time, all my brothers were settled in their jobs. Strangely, the National College legacy also continued. My fourth brother Madhura Babu left the job at the college and joined the State Bank of India in an officer's post (It is the biggest bank owned by the government of India and the agent of the government), and my fifth brother Ramatheertha joined the college in his place as economics lecturer!! Also, my sister Ramadevi, the youngest of my elder sisters, got married.

Consequently, my mother shifted to a smaller house in Machilipatnam by herself. But my house used to be full of hustle and bustle with her grandsons, granddaughters, and other relatives thronging to it. Our poverty never came in the way of anybody coming and staying there as long as they wanted. Even to this day, I am not able to understand how nobody thought anything of it. Perhaps, my mother managed it that way! That way – but how?? …..It is beyond my grasp.

As I knew well the difficulties at home and of my mother, I never used to waver in my studies but sincerely focused on them. My biggest entertainment those days was watching an NTR movie (NTR is an acronym for Nandamuri Taraka Ramarao, the thespian of the Telugu film Industry. He was more like a demi-god for the Telugu audience. He eventually entered politics. More of this later). Another habit was to clandestinely taste the food in the lunch boxes of my classmates. But this never exceeded the limits.

When I got fatigued by continuous study, I used to visit Sri Lakshmi Narayana Temple in Kurnool (Lord Narayana is one of the triumvirates of the Hindu pantheon along with Lord Brahma and Lord Shiva. Goddess Lakshmi is his consort, thus the name of the temple). Four miles away from the town of Kurnool on Kurnool-Anantapur road was a small but thick forest. Amidst that was a pond. On the banks of it was a Lord Shiva temple. There were no crowds. I used to go there on my bicycle, sit in a secluded place silently, and pray to the God. Except for the occasional chirping of birds, it was a very tranquil place. Many a time, only when it became dark, did I set out for the town. It was a great feeling of being very proximate to the God.

Similarly, on the banks of River Tungabhadra near Kurnol town, there was a Saibaba temple (a Hindu prophet and philosopher from India who worked for universal love and religious harmony, now deified as a God). That may have been the first Saibaba temple in the southern part of India. Some of his relics were on display there. Whenever possible, I used to go there. After worshipping Baba, if I sat on the steps of the temple, I could see the serene Tungabhadra river. Whatever I wished for at those holy places, I would achieve. That temple has strong divine powers. Even today, I have a great deal of faith about the temple.

Medical Colleges are known for student union elections and politics. But I always used to be faction agnostic and was known as a gentleman – good to one and all. The leadership qualities I had manifested during our admission days brought me a nickname of "Chanakya" (Chanakya was like an Indian Machiavelli, but with a relatively positive connotation. In fact, he belongs to a much earlier period than Machiavelli, circa B.C. 31. He was instrumental in establishing the Mauryan kingdom which ruled almost the entire India.) Hence, any and every problem was being brought to my notice. However, I used to come up with a solution that was above politics.

* Niccolò Machiavelli was an Italian philosopher who wrote the political treatise "The Prince," circa 1500, that encourages "the end justifies the means" behavior, especially among politicians.

But there was one incident that took place in my final year that
topped it all.

It was mandatory to pass all the four subjects in one go in the final year; those were medicine, surgery, gynecology, and public health (i.e., preventive medicine). If somebody fails in any of one of those subjects, then he is not eligible for admission into post-graduate courses. This created a kind of strange relationship between the students and the professors.

Our public health professor at that time was a kind of a wrangler. It was rumored in the campus that he was a sadist and intentionally failed a few students every year. In my final year, our cohort also had come to learn of this.

My classmates approached me stating, "This professor will certainly fail some of us. Do something to save us, my dear Chanakya!" So, we came up with a strategy. We found out what he liked. He was a food

lover and also he liked to speak at conferences. "Like" was a euphemism for his weaknesses. Therefore, throughout the year, we conducted several conferences and made him the central figure. He would get all the limelight. During those occasions, we would give him special food, baskets of fruits, sweets, etc. We also used to send baskets to his house.

Within six months, our cohort had carved a niche in his heart.

"Boys! It is very difficult to get sincere students nowadays and rare to see a group like yours," he praised us, immersed in his happiness. He also used to like me a lot.

On the day of our results, I was at Shankar Mutt of

Vidyanagar in Hyderabad. I was anxious about the results, not only about mine, but about the entire group. I prayed silently to Goddess Sharada, the Goddess of learning.

I felt relieved when I found out that my entire cohort was able to successfully pass the subject of Public Health. Our professor did not fail anyone and praised our cohort in front of everybody else. Subsequent cohorts got wind of my strategy. The next 4 to 5 cohorts followed the same modus operandi successfully.

Thus, I was able to successfully complete my studies in medicine in Kurnool Medical College in December 1971.

Chapter 5

A FRIEND IN NEED IS A FRIEND INDEED!

In January 1972, I entered my post-graduate program in medicine (M.D.) in Osmania University. I did my internship in Gandhi hospital. Those days the stipend was about Rs. 50 (less than $1 U.S.).

I stayed at my elder brother Madhura Babu's place at Himayat Nagar, Hyderabad. From there I used to travel to both college and hospital by city bus. Because of the erratic schedules of city buses, I used to often arrive late. In the hospital my professor was very strict. He used to start his rounds of the wards by 8 a.m. sharp. If anybody was late, he used to reprimand them very loudly in front of everybody. Although I used to arrive late quite often, I used to escape his reprimands.

Instead, he used to praise my discipline and demeanor in front of everybody. He used to tell other students, "See! You should learn from Dattu. If he is delayed, he sincerely informs me and arrives at the stroke of the promised minute." No sooner would he leave, than my classmates were about to pounce upon me in rage!

Dr. (Ms.) Kameswari Devi was our Obstetrics and Gynecology professor. About 40 to 50 pregnant women were in the obstetrics unit. Every day we were to do blood tests and report the hemoglobin level of each of them. My classmate Sitaram Prasad was lazy and used to frown on this: "Who would do that every day especially early in the morning before clinical rounds?" Therefore, he came up with a short cut method: He used to examine their eyes and tongue and estimate their approximate hemoglobin levels and document them accordingly in the chart.

Somehow Prof. Kameswari Devi grew suspicious about his notations. She wanted to know from me as to what he was doing. But, as a gentleman, I could only mumble without answering anything. But she was not to relent. So, she asked the patients directly, "Is he drawing blood from you?" Some answered in the affirmative, some in the negative, but certainly they were confused. So, he resorted to a new idea. Every day, he would draw their blood with a needle and document some approximate values in the chart without properly testing. We were amazed by his innovative methods of trickery.

Similarly, we used to resort to several tricks whenever we were assigned any night duty. What I can recollect is that we never used to

sleep on the cot meant for us, but only beneath it so that the nurses on duty could not find us when they required our signatures, so we could sleep soundly without getting disturbed. At the same time, we used to inform somebody to wake us up in case of any emergency! So, there was no mishap of any kind. If any nurse, nevertheless, complained to the professor, we used to tell him, "We went to have tea at that time, Sir!" and evade any admonition.

My intention in narrating these incidents is not to set any wrong examples for this generation, but to depict how at that age everyone indulges in such mischievous behavior. But that does not mean that we had any apathy towards the patients or disrespect for our medical profession.

The post-graduate program in medicine (Doctor of Medicine, M.D.) was a three-year course. I was keen to do surgery. But unfortunately, the Mulki and Non-Mulki agitation had gained momentum at that time. (Mulk is country/state. Those who belonged to Hyderabad or the former Telangana districts were called Mulkis, or Natives; others from other districts of combined Andhra Pradesh were called Non-Mulkis, or Non-Natives. Telangana was a cluster of districts which were under earlier Nizam rule before those were included in the Union of India after Indian independence.) Mulkis were given priority in admissions into surgery, the rest of us were bundled into oncology.

At that time, I could not realize that this was a turning point in my life! God willed otherwise. But my first love was surgery. Hence, I tried my best to get admission into a surgery program elsewhere. In fact, I clandestinely went to Delhi to take an entrance exam at Delhi University.

Why clandestinely? Because Doctor/Prof. Krishna Mohan Rao of oncology loved his students, even more so, me.

Somehow, he felt that I would come up well in that department. He resided near my place in Nallakunta (an area in Hyderabad city). One day, on his way, he inquired of my wife, Subhadra, "Where is Dattu? I haven't seen him at the college." But my wife innocently told him that I went to Delhi to take the entrance exam to obtain admission into surgery.

Despite my sincere attempts, I could not get a seat there either. Locals dominated there also.

Dr. Vasireddi Chandrasekhar Prasad was my classmate while I worked on my M.D. He became my close friend.

He was from Vadlamoodi village of the Guntur district. He did his degree in medicine in Belgaum, Karnataka. Before his joining his M.D. program, he married into a rich family. His father-in-law, Mr. Paruchuri Shivaprasad, owned a film distribution company that used to distribute National Art Theater films. After living for a few years in Chennai, he moved to Hyderabad. A relative of Chandrasekhar's in-laws was N. Trivikrama Rao. His brother was the late NTR (N. T. Ramarao), the demi-god of Telugus and the matinee idol turned politician, the former Chief Minister of the combined state of Andhra Pradesh. NTR used to frequent their house. Those days, I was thrilled to see my favorite hero nearby, but never ever imagined that in the future I would be working with him to accomplish a gargantuan project!

I used to go to my friend's house every day and from there together by car to M.N.J. Cancer Institute where we were doing our post-graduate
M.D. training.

Both Chandrasekhar and I did not show much interest in the M.D. program because we did not have much choice in being assigned to that department. So, we used to go to Hotel Sarovar near the Tank Bund (an area in Hyderabad) and voraciously eat either snacks or meals and contemplate what to do in the future.

By that time, his brother-in-law (the brother of Chandra's wife, Rajyalakshmi) Paruchuri Surendra Prasad was in the U.S. after completing his medicine degree. Chandrasekhar would receive up- to-date information in the field of medicine from his brother-in-law. One day my friend proposed, "Dattu! The radiology departments in our country are in a very primitive stage. If we want to improve them, we may have to go to the U.S. and work there for some time to learn new things." His words had a deep impact on me and inspired me to study in the U.S.

In those days to go to the U.S., it was mandatory for Indian medical students to pass the U.S. ECFMG (Educational Commission for Foreign Medical Graduates) exam. But the site to take the exam at that time was at Kuala Lumpur, Malaysia.

I did not have any money for either the fee or for the travel. Somehow, I was very reluctant to ask my brothers who had had done their best to take care of my upbringing and education. When I shared the information about the ECFMG exam with my father-in-law, Mr. Tadepalli Srinivasa Rao, he said, "Very good," but did not inquire about my finances regarding the exam. But, when I shared my predicament with Chandrasekhar, he promised me and assured me, "I will bear the expenses!"

I must share what happened during that time. When Subhadra, my wife (more about her and my marriage with her in the "Family" section), and I were struggling to adjust our finances for me to take the exam, Subhadra's father, my father-in-law, came home. There is an adage in my mother tongue, "Even one's own mother doesn't serve, unless one requests." So I thought if directly requested, my father-in-law might help me. I, therefore, pushed Subhadra to ask her father to fund my exam expenses. But she was so shy that she could not raise the issue at all.

After a brief chat, my father-in-law went away. Upon my compelling her, Subhadra ran after him. By that time, he had already crossed 2 or 3 by lanes. Finally, she caught up with him. After listening to the whole story, he gave her some money. Had he a mind to, he could have funded the exam fee and my entire expenses as well. But why he did not do it, I still can not understand.

Anyway, Chandrasekhar and I prepared together for the ECFMG exam. He had a good grip on some subjects; I was strong in some others. So we helped each other in preparation. We went to Kuala Lumpur for the exam via Madras (now Chennai).

Coincidentally, our seats were side by side in the same exam hall in spite of the authorities rearranging the rows in the examination hall many times. So, we were able to attend the exam without any fear. As promised, he bore all my expenses. His father-in-law, Mr. Paruchuri Shivaprasad, also liked me and helped both of us a great deal.

We got through the exam with flying colors. After the exam, each of us bought a "two-in-one" audio system. When we went to Madras while returning from Malaysia, we also saw the film shooting of my favorite film hero, NTR (N. T. Ramarao).

By that time, we had not yet completed our M.D. course. But my friend Chandrasekhar discontinued his M.D. program and left for the U.S. six months earlier than I. Unlike him, I was not financially sound. I, therefore, had decided to go to the U.S. only after my completion of my M.D.

Turning point

While working on my M. D., I was able to get an assignment as a resident at Radium Institute and Cancer Hospital near Red Hills in Hyderabad.

There, I witnessed a few blood curdling scenes.

We had a radiation room there: Every day, 15 to 20 patients of gynecological cancer, lined up on beds, were receiving internal radiation while we were attending them, standing amidst them. Standing next to one patient with a radioactive element significantly exposes the professional staff member. Since that is the case, just imagine the level of exposure standing amidst the whole group of patients receiving radiation. In this situation, healthy doctors and nurses used to get exposed to the detrimental effects of radiation. The patients also ran the risk of side effects on the healthy parts of their bodies and suffered endlessly. I was troubled by this primitive technique.

During that brief period, I saw first hand the devastating, devouring effect of cancer. I was determined to change treatment for the better to a modern technique on par with the ones used in advanced countries such as the U.S.

Hyderabad Osmania University conducted an international conference. One group of doctors came from the U.S. to attend it. My professor entrusted me to assist them. I did my best that whole week to be of help to the guests in their work. They enlightened us about the very impactful modern treatment techniques they had been adopting in the U.S. to tackle cancer. The leader of that group was the head of a department at Sloan-Kettering Memorial Hospital in America. He was very impressed with my academic caliber and leadership qualities. Before returning, he gave me his business card and told me, "Dr. Nori, if you happen to come to the U.S., meet me without fail." I never knew that this moment would change my life.

What I understood was that the U.S. was miles ahead of us in cancer treatment. This dominated my thought process. I became so determined to learn the modern methods of treatment. Also firmly seeded in my mind was the goal that if I studied the American treatment techniques that it would help Indian patients as well. My friend Chandrasekhar's encouragement further boosted this dream. In fact, he also funded my U.S. journey!

I set out in June 1976 to the U.S., leaving my family behind in Hyderabad. My son, Sateesh, was hardly 3 months old. I landed in the New York airport with $15 in my pocket. I was granted a Green Card as soon as I landed there. I went to my cousins Malladi Shastry and Nirmala's place. No hospital was ready to give me a residency or job there as they thought that I was overqualified. "You have already done your M.D., and you would not stay with us for long," was the routine refrain I encountered. It was very painful. About 45 days passed but to no avail. Somehow, I was able to get a temporary assignment in Brooklyn's Long Island College Hospital. I stayed in an apartment provided by them.

By God's grace, I then recalled that I had the business card of the professor from Sloan-Kettering Memorial Hospital. I took it out and called his phone number. They had had a fellowship, but by that time, it was already assigned to somebody from the Philippines.

"You could have called me as soon as you landed here, Dr. Nori!" said the professor. However, he still called me in for an interview. If the candidate to whom that fellowship was already assigned failed to turn up by July 4, they would call me on July 5 and, then, I should immediately join them. I agreed to the proposition as I was left with no other option.

During that period, my mind precariously oscillated like a pendulum between hope and despair. I was very tense and anxious. I prayed to every God.

with my best friend at my daughter 's sweet 16 celebration L- R Dr Vasi Reddy Chandrashekar and his wife, Smt. Rajya Lakshmi, my daughter Priya Nori.

Finally, they called the residence of my cousins. Fortunately, my cousin received the call and contacted me by phone in Brooklyn. I was to report and by that evening join Memorial Sloan-Kettering.

I was able to complete my work by in Brooklyn by 2 pm.

I had only ten dollars with me. I gathered courage to call a cab to go to Sloan-Kettering. The driver told me that it would cost me ten dollars. I had on me an opened milk carton and yogurt that I had just bought. He looked at me askance and chided me, "I can't allow you to carry milk and yogurt into my cab as I am afraid that you may spill them." He continued, ridiculing me, "Won't you be able to get them in Manhattan?"

"No, my dear friend! I know that everything is available in Manhattan, but if I throw them out here, after paying my last dollar to you," I lamented and explained with all sincerity, "I will not have anything to buy any more again."

He, perhaps, felt sorry for me and allowed me to board with a statement of caution, "Hold them properly and carefully so that you won't spill them in the vehicle."

When my cab journey ended, he dropped me in front of the renowned Memorial Sloan-Kettering Cancer Center in New York.

Chapter 6

WORLD CLASS INSTITUTIONS- WORLD CLASS LEARNING

Manhattan is a very crowded place in New York. Memorial Sloan- Kettering Cancer Center (MSK) is situated there. Across from it lies New York Hospital (Cornell University Medical College). Both are world-renowned institutions and housed in multiple buildings. Looking at them, my head had a spin. In that confused state of mind, I went into the reception area of New York Hospital, Cornell Medical Center, instead of that of MSK. Perhaps, destiny wanted it that way. Although from there, they guided me to MSK, I did not have any inkling that I was destined to hold top positions in both institutions.

Memorial Sloan Kettering Cancer Center is not an ordinary organization. By then, it already had a long history of its own. This is the oldest and the largest private cancer center in the world.

Initially in 1884, it started as New York Cancer Hospital in the Manhattan area of New York. John Jacob Astor III and his wife Charlotte founded it. William B. Coley was working as the attending surgeon. He belonged to the first generation of doctors who tackled tumors with immunotherapy. In 1899 the hospital had become General Memorial Hospital. Its objective was to treat cancer and allied ailments.

Prof. James Ewing from Cornell Medical College established collaboration with Memorial Hospital in 1910. An industrialist by the name of James Douglas, in those days, donated 100,000 U.S. dollars towards clinical research. Such funding provided for the lab required for the active evaluation of radium's role and further research on radio therapy as well as 20 beds.

With the charity of Mr. Rockefeller, the first fellowship program started in the hospital in 1927. In 1931 the 900kv x-ray tube was used in radio therapy for cancer treatment. In the same year Mr. James Irving became the president of the hospital.

The prestigious "Time" magazine carried a story "Cancer Man Irving" with his picture on its cover. By the time he retired after 9 years, Memorial Hospital topped all the hospitals in the

United States.

New York Presbyterian Hospital in Manhattan, New York

While addressing the treatment of patients, it gained name and fame in clinical research and lab diagnostics.

In 1934, John D. Rockefeller donated some land on York Avenue and after 2 years, 3 million U.S. dollars to the hospital. From then onwards, the hospital was moved to a new location.

In 1945, Alfred P. Sloan, the then Chairman of General Motors, donated 4 million US dollars; the vice-president of the same company, Mr. Kettering came forward to support the research of the hospital. Thus, Sloan-Kettering Institute for Cancer Research was established.

After 3 years, Cornelius P. Rhoads became the director of the hospital. "During World War II, he worked for the United States Army helping to develop chemical weapons and set up research centers. Research on mustard gas (nitrogen mustard) led to developments for its use in chemotherapy at Sloan-Kettering.

Along with a few more clinicians, he also discovered a medicine called 6mp, among his many other accomplishments. In brief, Memorial Hospital continued its journey ahead of others in cancer research in the 1950s and '60s, including pediatric oncology. So many donors, doctors, and researchers collaborated in that endeavor. The organization felt that it was not enough to merely treat cancer but also necessary to provide mental fortitude to concerned patients and, hence, started an exclusive department. It was a pioneering initiative, indeed. During treatment and after recovery also, experts would equip patients with a great deal of courage.

In the early '70s, when the U.S. declared war on Cancer, three hospitals were declared as "Comprehensive Cancer Centers." Memorial Sloan-Kettering was one of the three. With the amalgamation of Memorial Hospital and Sloan-Kettering Institute in 1980 was born Memorial Sloan-Kettering Cancer Center. Year after year, MSK is considered as the number one cancer center in the U.S.

Thereafter, for the last 50 years, this organization has been progressing in all respects. As of now, about 1,000 doctors are working at MSK and about 400 types of cancers are being treated there. Every year 600,000 people avail themselves of treatment in the center. The number of researchers also runs into thousands, and there is no dearth of donors who support it.

Fellowship

When I saw that organization and set my foot inside, I was not sure whether it was a dream or reality because that was the first time in my life I was seeing a world-renowned cancer institute of that stature. I decided to work hard, conduct topnotch research in cancer at this institute and help cancer patients world over.

The radiation oncology department of this reputed hospital, Memorial Sloan-Kettering, was headed by a Chinese scientist and physician named Dr. Florence Chu as its chairperson. Her story is a very inspiring one.

Dr. Chu graduated in medicine in 1942 from the National College of Shanghai. The same year, the Japanese occupied that area of her country. Hence, her college was shifted to another area called Chunking. She did her training in radiology there for 3 years. After the Second World War, the Chinese government wanted to send some of its students abroad for higher studies. Having cleared the relevant exam, therefore, Dr. Chu and her husband came to the U.S. in 1947. Thereafter, the communist revolution took China by storm and came into power. Because of these developments, Dr. Chu and her husband could not return to their country. She came to Memorial Sloan-Kettering as a special fellow in January 1949 and worked there for the next 38 years. She rose to become the chair of the Radiation department. After retirement from MSK, she continued to work there until she attained her 80th birthday.

Dr. Chu interviewed me. Two and a half weeks later, in the first week of July 1976, I joined the Department of Radiation Oncology at MSK as a special fellow. Normally, residency is mandatory to obtain the fellowship, but as I had completed my M.D. in India, I was offered a fellowship directly. Otherwise, I would have had to complete 3 years residency training first. It was beneficial that I already had my M.D. I would get a fellowship stipend of 600 U.S. dollars per month.
MSK also allocated an apartment for my stay.

On the very first day of my commencing my duties, I didn't have any money. I would not get my fellowship stipend until the end of the month. I met a few people who were part of the Telugu diaspora and explained my predicament. They gave me $10 with which I could manage.

After 3 months, my wife Subhadra and my son, Sateesh, came to the U.S. By then, my son was 8 months old. When I wanted to take him into my arms, he started crying as he did not recognize me. It took a few days for him to get comfortable with me. For their journey and essential provisions for our home, I borrowed 1,000 U.S. dollars from Dr. Ravipati and was able to repay him within the next 2 to 3 months.

Bond worthier than the gold

But what I could never repay, but make only a token gesture towards, was what my mother did for me in particular, for my kith and kin in general.

As I was the last child in the house, I always spent more time with my mother and observed firsthand the personal sacrifices she made to help the family.
One particular event disturbed me a lot.

As briefly mentioned above, as we had no sources of income, she was concerned about how to pay the tuition fee for the education of one of my brothers, so to pay the tuition fee, she decided to sell her gold bangles, the only jewelry she ever had all through her life.

This event had disturbed my mind throughout my education period. I was determined that in the future when I would become employed, I would buy her a new pair of gold bangles with my first paycheck and present them to her.

When I received my first month's salary from Memorial Sloan Kettering, I went to an Indian Jewelry shop in New York and bought her a beautiful pair of gold bangles and presented them to her during my very first trip to India. She was so happy to wear them and showed them to all my relatives. I felt immensely happy and my eyes became wet with tears that I had made good on my wish to make her wear gold bangles again.

I went all the way to Hyderabad and adorned her hands with them, and in the happiness, I could see on her face that day, assets of millions of dollars simply fade away. She proudly told everyone -- those who inquired, and those who did not -- "My son Dattu brought these bangles for me from America."

Frankly speaking…

I have not yet told you the name of the gentleman who had given me his visiting card when I was working in MNJ Cancer Hospital in Hyderabad and asked me to meet him when I visited the U.S.

His name is Dr. Frank Ellis. He was the chairman of the department of Radiation Oncology at Memorial Sloan-Kettering Hospital. When I first joined MSK, people there were astonished to know that he had left his business card with me. It was not an ordinary thing, so their impression was that if such a highly placed man left his card with this young man, perhaps Dr. Ellis thought that radiation would be this young doctor's métier. In fact, Dr. Ellis was very powerful and had more credibility than the president of the institute itself. Dr. Ellis was from England. In 1943 when the first Radiotherapy department was started at Royal London Hospital, he was its first director. After he retired in 1970 in his country, he was appointed as a visiting professor at both the University of Southern California and Memorial Sloan-Kettering Hospital in New York.

Dr Frank Ellis, my mentor and teacher who helped with my transition to the U.S.

He was totally devoted to discovering the ideal dose of radiation that should be administered to eradicate malignant tumors without impacting healthy cells. He was responsible for determining the "Nominal Standard Dose." This paved the way for standardization of the dose across hospitals internationally.

He came to India in 1974. By then, he was a consultant to the World Health Organization as well as to the International Atomic Energy Agency. He had come to Hyderabad to participate in an international conference on "The innovative methods to be developed in the developing countries." That was when I was entrusted to take care of his delegation. That was the time when I made my presentation which he saw and liked too. Hence, he left his business card with me, asking me to meet him when I would be in the U.S., when even visiting
-- forget working and settling there. At that time, the U.S. was not even a remote dream for me.

From my days of fellowship, he treated me very well and encouraged me. Although he was at the acme of his career, Dr. Ellis believed that every new patient was a new challenge. He didn't believe in the theory: "Same medicines and same treatment for all patients." He would treat every patient with special care.

His illustrious life in medicine and research inspired many a student and trainee.

Winning accolades and awards, he lived his 100 years of life to the fullest He was an embodiment of enthusiasm, creativity, and immense love for humanity. He was a wonderful person. It is not hyperbole to call him the world leader in radiation therapy for cancer. He founded many organizations. His fame has been well entrenched by the Royal College of Radiologists through its introduction of annual speeches and a medal named after him.

Once, I organized a party in his honor in New York and invited doctors and others closely known to both of us. By then, he was 95.

Another time, while we were travelling by car, he said to me, "Dr. Nori, we should conduct some research on the trees by the side of the highways. While so many vehicles are bombarding them with pollutants, how are they able to endure it? If we can find out what property is giving them that strength, humans at large can benefit further." As a doctor and a human being, that was the noble concern he had had for humans!!

I was fortunate to be guided by such "Gurus" and to spend many years in their August company. His life, spanning from 1905 until 2006, was very productive, and he was active until very close to his death at the age of 100.

The rise to the acme of my achievement in my professional name, fame, and progress can be largely attributed to him, and it was his business card that he gave to me in Hyderabad that laid the initial path to glory!

After my fellowship, in the third year, I became an attending doctor. By 1979, I earned the certification/accreditation of the American Board of Therapeutic Radiology (New York State License). Later, I advanced to the next level as Assistant Attending and Assistant Professor of Radiation Oncology.

Beginning as an assistant doctor, then an associate doctor, I thereafter became a professor. Meanwhile, my wife Subhadra also completed her residency and obtained a position. On October 27, 1980, my daughter was born as our second child, whom we named Priya. Taking care of both Sateesh and Priya while both of us were working made our lives very hectic and the time flew.

During this time, in 1980, my brother Ramatheerdha came to New York during his return journey to India from Warsaw (Poland) where he went for some training course. He was the first visitor to my house in New York and it was a very happy moment for our family.

Chapter 7

BABY STEPS IN BRACHYTHERAPY

The fellowship I was able to obtain in New York was in Brachytherapy. "Brachy" is a Greek word which means short or small. Brachytherapy delivers the radiation precisely to the area of cancer in the body to destroy those cells. This therapy has a long history.

Before dealing with that concept, let us try to understand what radiation is. Those who have studied science may already be familiar with the topic. But even laypersons can also easily understand it. About 100 years ago, scientists discovered that certain elements of nature emit very powerful rays. Sir William Crooks experimented and discovered "Cathode Rays" in 1850. While the German scientist Philipp Lenard found that cathode rays can be used for photography, another German scientist, Wilhelm Rontgen, discovered the X-Rays that could permeate the body and show the inside picture!

Thereafter research about the myriad usages of different kinds of rays continued. But the most notable research was by the couple – Madame Marie Skłodowska Curie popularly known as Madame Marie Curie and her husband Mr. Pierre Curie. Being a woman did not deter her. The Curies did not have well-equipped labs or adequate funds; moreover, the French press always used to look at her with suspicion as she was a refugee from Poland. Despite all odds, undaunted, the couple focused themselves on the research.

They discovered an active element 300 times more powerful than Uranium. Madam /curie named it after her motherland as "Polonium." They found that the unstable atomic nucleus of Polonium unleashes this energy, and Madam Curie called it "Radioactivity" (a term she coined).

Their successful discoveries gave them further encouragement to continue their research and they found an element 900 times more active than Uranium: That was "Radium."

["She shared the 1903 Nobel Prize in Physics with her husband Pierre Curie and physicist Henri Becquerel, for their pioneering work developing the theory of "radioactivity". Using techniques she invented for isolating radioactive isotopes, she won the 1911 Nobel Prize in Chemistry for the discovery of two elements, polonium and radium.

Madame Curie was the first woman to win a Nobel Prize, the first person and the only woman to win the Nobel Prize twice, and the only person to win the Nobel Prize in two scientific fields. She was also the first woman to become a professor at the University of Paris"- (Wikipedia)]

The scientists who discovered X-Ray and Radiation have done a great deal of good for the human race at large. These discoveries were turning points in the field of medicine. We shall, therefore, always remember them.

The doctors who have found out that radioactive elements destroy cancer cells are no less important. Dr. H. Strebel from Munich was the first doctor who successfully used radiation treatment. It was the first step towards Brachytherapy.

In 1903, the inventor of the telephone, Alexander Graham Bell, in a letter to a magazine called "American Medicine" exhorted doctors to do research on targeting the rays to permeate tissue straight towards the cancerous tumors, as radiation otherwise kills even healthy cells.

A year before that Pierre Curie asked Dr. Henry Dunlose to arrange radium in a small tube and radiate directly to the cancerous tumors. That was the first step towards the current "Intra-cavitary Brachytherapy." Experiments continued in this line of treatment. With every success, treatment progressed one step forward. In 1931, Dr. G. Forssel used the term "Brachytherapy" for the first time.

Doctors continued the experiments as to how much radioactive element should be used, what kind of catheters or capsules would be better, etc. Another challenge was to protect the impact of radiation on the healthy doctors, technicians and nursing staff. It is not out of place to mention that Madam Curie who discovered "radioactivity" became a victim of it. ["Marie Curie died in 1934, aged 66, at a sanitorium in Sancellemoz (Haute-Savoie), France of aplasticanaemia from exposure to radiation in the course of her scientific research and in the course of her radiological work at field hospitals during World War I"(Wikipedia)]. Although External Beam Radiation (EBT) has been progressively improved and has been working efficaciously, scientists have not stopped searching for solutions for both of the above problems.

In 1930 Irene Juliet, daughter of the Curies, and their son-in-law, Frederick, discovered artificial radio activity elements. Instead of the potentially dangerous elements such as radium, etc., the usage of those alternatives was introduced.

In 1960 Dr. Ulrich Henschke* and Dr. Basil S. Hilaris developed "After Loading" devices. By which both above-mentioned problems have been almost solved. Those two gentlemen were my "Gurus" in Brachytherapy, and they trained me to be an expert in the domain.

*"Ulrich Henschke was noted for mechanical efforts to put exact amounts of ionizing radiation into the tumors of his patients. Notable to those who saw his demonstrations of brachytherapy in the 1960s were 'after loading devices' to insert radon or artificial isotopes into cervical or uterine cancers" (JACR). The students of the subject used to stand in queues to watch him working on Brachytherapy patients. "After loading" is a very complex concept. "The concept was to position applicators without the radiation sources. Then, using air pressure or hydraulics, the sources would be forced into place and then withdrawn after the intended doses were delivered. The combination of metal fittings, pumps, and rubber tubes leading from radiation safes to the applicators in patients added an unusual touch to a very serious solution to a difficult problem" (JACR). To organize the whole thing meticulously was not an ordinary task.

All this experimentation was not an easy walk through, even for Dr. Henschke. For a long time, doctors never used to believe that cancer cells could be destroyed by radiation. He was to wage several battles to vindicate and prove his stand on radiation therapy.

Ulrich Henschke was born in 1914 in Germany in a family of scientists. He obtained his Ph.D. both in medicine and physics from the University of Berlin. After World War II, he was invited by the U.S. After working for some time in Memorial

Sloan Kettering Cancer Center, he left for Howard University, which was dealing with several African countries. He was instrumental in starting 9 cancer centers in 10 countries in Africa. He encouraged the students from those countries. During one of his frequent trips to Africa, in June 1980, a small plane in which he was travelling crashed, and he died in the accident. He was only 66. Because of that tragedy, my association with him was brief, but nevertheless fruitful. My other "Guru" in Brachytherapy was Dr. Basil S. Hilaris. **

**"Hilaris, Basil S., MD., was born in Athens, Greece on September 3rd, 1928 to Anna and Stavros Hilaris, with his childhood during World War II and the Greek Civil War. He went on to graduate from the National University of Athens Medical School in 1955 with his Medical Degree. The same year he immigrated to the United States, to the New York area and in 1957 he started working at Memorial Sloan Kettering Cancer Center as a Radiation Oncologist and was a Professor at the Weill Cornell Medical College. He was one of the pioneers in the field of Brachytherapy, "the insertion of Radioactive Seeds in the treatment of various forms of cancer". (www.frankpatti.com) By the time I joined MSK, he was already the chief of Brachytherapy B division there.

"Serving as Chief of the Brachytherapy Service, he was also a President of the American Brachytherapy Society and among his many awards, in 1996 he was the first recipient of the Marie Curie Gold Medal Award, presented for a major contribution in the development of the field of Brachytherapy. In 1988 he moved on to be Chairman of the Department of Radiation Medicine at New York Medical College and Our Lady of Mercy Medical Center until his retirement at the age of 80 in 2008. In addition, he was an author of many books in the field of Radiation Oncology and Brachytherapy. But his favorite pastime was his research and authoring of books about Greek History and Ancient to Present Greek Medicine." (www.frankpatti.com)

Brachytherapy has made unimaginable strides of progress from those days. Before this therapy became accepted, had any part of the body become cancerous, more often than not, the line of treatment was removing that part of the body by surgery.

The latter practice used to wreak heavy pain and anguish on

patients. With the progress of Brachytherapy, most of those problems are addressed. Similarly, the side effects and the impact healthy cells by radiation have also disappeared. The cost of Brachytherapy is very marginal when compared to the conventional mode of treatment. The time duration spent on treatment is also short. Patients need not stay in the hospital for a long time, which also saves costs for treatment. In fact, in the recent past, we have started providing most Brachytherapy treatment on an out-patient basis. Consequently, patients' regular lifestyle is also not disrupted. The very next day, they can resume their job duties, or regular activities.

My Innovation

I have made further progress by combining both Brachytherapy and modern technology – especially using computers. It is not an exaggeration if I claim that it has elevated cancer treatment one more step. By using computers, we are able to decimate even the tumors that are very small in size, and not easily visible to the naked eye. Whichever part of the body is affected by cancer such as the cervix, prostrate, breast, esophagus, or skin, Brachytherapy can be employed to cure it.

On the 100th year of introduction of Brachytherapy in 2005, I wrote a book on the subject. Its title is "Brachytherapy for Cancer, a resource guide for patients." The main objectives of the book were to explain what Brachytherapy is, how it works on different affected parts of the body, and how to prepare a patient for treatment, and imbue them with courage.

Also, several patients who have been cured by Brachytherapy and lived for decades longer shared their experiences in this book.

Writing the Preface, well-known Dr. Kakarla Subbarao opined, "I really liked documenting the experiences of the patients. It is very important. It could be used like an encyclopedia to understand both cancer and Brachytherapy. The book mirrors the sincerity of Dr. Nori Dattatreyudu towards his profession as well as his commitment to give a new life to his patients.

Basil's leaf

D. Basil S. Hilaris, the chief of my department suffered a heart attack in 1979. He was, consequently, constrained to take about 6 or 7 months leave. As his disciple and associate chief of service, I took over all his work. I had tried to do my best however difficult it was. I used to draft his speeches to which he had had already committed before his stroke and also attend conferences as his representative. Thus, I was able to gain a good understanding of and experience with other major cancer centers in the U.S. and the world.

MSK used to conduct international conferences as a legacy. In the absence of Dr. Basil S. Hilaris, I worked very hard to conduct such conferences. During those 6 to 7 months, 15 to 20 international conferences took place, and each of them had 400 to 500 doctors from various countries as participants. Professors from the most reputed institutions in the U.S. used to request that we allow them to participate in those conferences.

I believe that one's hard work only becomes one's experience and takes one to places. My efforts did not go to waste. Thereafter, backed by that experience, along with Dr. Basil S. Hilaris, I was able to write several books on Brachytherapy and Cancer. Those works were of immense use for a number of doctors, students, and patients across the world.

From Dr. Basil to Dr. Beattie

While I was a fellow with Dr. Basil S. Hilaris, I also used to work with Dr. Edward James Beattie and his patients. He was a renowned chest surgeon, lung cancer expert, and a professor. A doctor with a great character, he inspired surgeons, medical oncologists, and radiation oncologists to be on the same page and work in unison about their patients. He was the first oncologist in the world to introduce the concept of multidisciplinary cancer care. He invented several new modes of treatment for lung cancer. He treated many important people as well. He was the founder of Miami University Cancer Center.

Dr. Beattie was born in Philadelphia and completed his M.D at Harvard medical School. From 1965 until his stepping down from his administrative role in 1983, for 18 years he worked as Chief Medical Officer at Memorial Hospital. Thereafter, he has relentlessly worked to establish exclusive centers for lung cancer treatment.

Such a great man was my "Guru" professionally. He liked me like his own son. He paved the way for my progress. He loved India. In India, Memorial Sloan-Kettering, where we worked, had earned a huge reputation as a great hospital. Hence, every Indian politician and celebrity who needed cancer treatment used to come to MSK.

It was a favorite pastime for Dr. Beattie to know about India and to talk to those Indian patients who had had come to MSK for treatment. After the treatment, if any one invited him, he was very eager to go to India. He had come along with me many a time. During one of those trips, one funny incident took place.

About 15 to 20 U.S. doctors came to Mumbai as a group to attend an international conference on cancer and stayed in Hotel Oberoi. Most of them would take a little wine or whisky during their supper time. While Dr. Beattie was leisurely sipping his drink, we were deep in conversation.

"We need a few instruments for our department, and it is better we buy them as soon as we return," I said to him.

"Oh, yes Datta! Let us certainly do that. Get your proposal ready," he nodded readily. I was on cloud nine to hear that.

Next morning, at the breakfast table, I initiated the dialogue, "I am preparing the proposals as we discussed last night."

addressing a doctor's group at an oncology meeting at MSKCC with Dr Harris and Dr.Fuks.

"Did we? What was that about? I don't remember any.... Can you tell me again?" was his response. I almost fainted that time!!

After my coming to the U.S, my personal life was a smooth cruise. Not that I did not have any money problems in my early days in the U.S. To share one instance, I purchased my first car for 175 U.S. dollars. It was pre-owned. While I was bringing it home, it came to a sudden halt and refused to move on an overpass. With the help of others, I was able to somehow park it on the side of the road. I went back to the seller and persuaded him to return my $175 after my strong argument with him as to how he could sell me such a vehicle.

Thereafter, I purchased another car for 250 U.S. dollars. This car was a good one. "Let us celebrate your purchasing a new car, let us visit Niagara Falls," insisted my friends. About 4 to 5 of us with our families set out, reached the Falls after a 10-hour drive, and checked into a hotel. Perhaps, an hour into my sleep, the hotel manager knocked on my door.

"Some inebriated driver could not properly drive and hence hit several cars in the parking area reducing 4 or 5 of them into shambles. Come and check whether your vehicles were involved," he coolly broke the news! I felt very heavy and agitated as I had bought the car.

only three days ago. I found that my car was heavily damaged. In those days, I was not well-versed about the provisions of insurance, etc. I really felt the pinch, and I was about to break down.

"Having come all the way, how can we skip Niagara? Whatever loss we have incurred, nothing can be done," we consoled one another and went to see the Falls. Perhaps our tears also flowed down them!!

Later, I left the car with a local acquaintance to get it repaired and returned to the hotel. On the way back, we found farmers selling fruits and vegetables from their farms. I found some nice eggplant (called "Brinjal" in India) and purchased three baskets of them. The farmer was surprised and inquired whether I owned a restaurant in New York. I explained the Indians liking for eggplant to him.

My friends insisted visiting one of their relative's houses on the way and having lunch there. The hostess there served us food with typical curry and Dal (pigeon pea). When my friends were all praise for the food and its taste, she, with a half-smile, boasted that the curry was prepared two years ago and was preserved in the deep freezer. She had taken it out just now, defrosted, heated, and served it. She was happy that my friends liked it.

Listening to this, I was about to vomit. I don't like to eat for supper what was prepared for lunch, so then, how could I relish the curry she had had prepared two years ago!

Chapter 8

PRESIDENT SRI NEELAM SANJIVA REDDY

Almost four decades ago, when the then president of India, Sri Neelam Sanjiva Reddy, prodded me, questioning, "What do you want, Doctor?", it was my naivety that caused me not to ask for anything. It is not that I am regretting it that I mention this, but to forewarn others not to make the same mistake.

Let me recall that honor and privilege of treating His Excellency, the then Hon. President of the biggest democracy in the world, The Republic of India.

H.E. Neelam Sanjiva Reddy was the sixth President of India. He was the youngest of them all as he became president when he was only 64. He was the first to be elected unopposed to that post. He held his full term of presidency from July 1977 until July 1982.

He had also served as the first chief minister of the integrated state of Andhra Pradesh (Vishal Andhra was carved out of combined Madras province in 1953. With the integration of the Telugu-speaking districts of Hyderabad [Nizam] State in 1956, it came to be known as Andhra Pradesh). He was also the speaker of Lok Sabha (the lower house of Parliament of India) and also rendered his services as a cabinet minister in the Union Government of India. He was born in the village of Illuru, in the district of Anantapur, earlier in the Madras presidency. He had actively participated in the Indian freedom struggle.

Holding several important positions in the state and the union of India, he was known to have a strong personality. The legend goes that he declined permission to world-renowned film director Sir Richard Attenborough to shoot his film "Gandhi" in the "Rashtrapathi Bhavan" (the residential suites of the president of India, which were designed by Sir Edwin Lutyens). He was also known to have formidably faced and countered a very strong prime minister and political personality, Ms. Indira Gandhi.

While he was the president of India, he went for an annual routine check-up to the All-India Institute of Medical Sciences (AIIMS) in New Delhi. Unexpectedly, a coin-like lesion was detected on the upper lobe of his left lung. The biopsy confirmed that he had lung cancer. The

with our past President Shri Neelam Sanjiva Reddy and Mrs. Reddy, after successful completion of treatment for lung cancer at Sloan-Kettering Cancer Center A unique Brachytherapy technique was designed by me for his treatment.

doctors there recommended his treatment at Memorial Sloan-Kettering Cancer Center in New York.

A coin-like lesion can appear on the lungs, but it isn't necessarily malignant. It can be benign as well. In addition, this tumor can appear in the lungs if there is cancer in any other part of the body. It can also be T.B. Or it might not be any of these. But, the probability of its turning into cancer is quite high. Therefore, often, radiologists try to investigate from that perspective and also start the treatment as quickly as possible.

Since the doctors at AIIMS recommended he be treated at world-renowned MSK hospital in New York, Mr. Sanjiva Reddy immediately came to the US. I was part of the group of doctors that treated him. Our acquaintance blossomed well during his brief stay there. Every day, when I would visit him, he would share with me his thoughts from his valuable life experience. His wisdom was worth preserving like treasured maxims. For example, he used to often say, "Children should not be left in baby care centers or to the care of the ayahs. Parents should personally take care of them."

He was also well known for his photographic/elephantine memory. I had the occasion to witness it. Mr. K.S.R. Moorthy was an IAS officer. He was a Telugu man hailing from the Godavari district of Andhra Pradesh. He had brought his wife Anasuya Devi* to MSK as she was suffering from lung cancer. I was treating her. When Mr. Neelam Sanjiva Reddy had been the Chief Minister of the integrated state of Andhra Pradesh, Mr. Moorthy had worked in his government. With that familiarity, he inquired of me whether he could meet with Mr. Reddy. I obliged his request and arranged the meeting in the hospital. Before meeting with him, Mr. Moorthy shared his lingering doubt with me as to whether Mr. Reddy would remember him! But surprisingly when he met with the president, the latter immediately greeted him by name, "Hello, Mr. Moorthy! How are you?" The president also recalled the services Mr. Moorthy had rendered, including the time period of his service and his then designation, etc. Why people praise Mr. Reddy's excellent memory was evident to both Mr. Moorthy and me.

*Anasuya Devi recovered and left for home. She lived long thereafter without any health problems. After retirement from his civil service, Mr. Moorthy joined the Indian National Congress, contested the elections, and entered the 11th Parliament's lower house as a member. He was the M.P. (Member of Parliament) representing the Amalapuram constituency of Andhra Pradesh (after G.M.C. Balayogi died in a helicopter crash while serving as the speaker of Lok Sabha).

Mr. Reddy, being the then President of the Indian Republic, several VIPs visited my hospital to see him and inquire about his health. I was entrusted to take care of such visitors too. Thus, during those days, I met several important people. Mr. Reddy recovered after an effective course of treatment and returned to "Rashtrapathi Bhavan" in India. I later used to meet him whenever I visited India. He would say to me, frankly, "Doctor, you are an excellent professional; you saved the life of the Indian

President." He then would ask, "As a gesture of goodwill, what do you want from the government of India? Any Padma award or any such high civilian award??"

"No, no, Sir, your affection and blessings are more than those awards." With a smile, such was my humble reaction.

Partly, perhaps, I did not realize the real significance of those honors; partly, I sincerely felt that his love for me was more than adequate thanks. Nevertheless, although I could have received those honors much before 1980, I allowed the opportunity to slip through my fingers.

After completing his term, Mr. Reddy shifted his residence to Bangalore, in the Southern state of Karnataka (adjacent to the state of Andhra Pradesh). After leaving the presidential suite, "Rashtrapathi Bhavan," he mostly used to spend his time, along with his wife Mrs. Nagaratnamma, either in Bangalore or in his farmhouse near Anantapur. He had a son and three daughters. Whenever his children would visit him with their families, he would be very happy. Sometimes, he used to stay in Hyderabad "Raj Bhavan," the official residence of the state governor. I would always meet him whenever I was in India, either in Hyderabad or Bangalore. On every such occasion, he arranged a sumptuous vegetarian feast for me.

Also, we had interesting conversations. If any of my brothers accompanied me in such visits, he used to affectionately tell them, "Your brother has given me life." After his treatment for cancer, he lived his life to the fullest for 14 long years. During that period, he penned and published his autobiography "From Farmhouse to Rashtrapathi Bhavan." At the age of 83, he died on June 1, 1996, purely due to geriatric causes.

Because I had treated the president of India, many celebrities and prominent people from India came to know about me.

Chapter 9

NASREEN BANU STATE BECKONS

I think it was in the last month of 1979, the name of one "Nasreen Banu" reverberated from Andhra Pradesh to the international level. Why was it so? What happened?

It was a serious error: medical negligence....an offense that cannot be reversed for a lifetime.

Nasreen Banu was a two-year-old girl. She hailed from a poor family of Hyderabad. Her father Bahadur Khan was not a literate man. He was a small-time mechanic. He had taken her for an eye ailment to the renowned government eye hospital of Hyderabad, Sarojini Devi Eye Hospital. Doctors examined her and found that the eye was affected by cancer. They wanted to remove it by performing surgery. The girl's parents admitted her to the hospital. As planned, the doctors performed the surgery.

When the child was brought out after surgery, her parents were shocked as the operation had been performed on the healthy eye! This meant that the child had become blinded for life.

The doctors' negligence had rendered Nasreen Banu's future bleak and dark. The news spread like wildfire. The government shuddered.

Not only did the press from Hyderabad cover her tragedy, but even the international papers carried headlines about it. Dr. Marri Chennareddy, the then Chief Minister of Andhra Pradesh, intervened. Someone reminded him about MSK, which had treated President Neelam Sanjiva Reddy. Perhaps, he was told about me also -- A Telugu- speaking doctor from the same state. He called me and spoke to me over the phone. I was astonished to know what had happened. "We shall certainly do everything that we are capable of," I assured him. Dr. Chennareddy immediately sent both Nasreen Banu and her father to New York at the expense of the government. They came to my house first. My heart melted as I saw that hapless child.

"I am an illiterate. Hence, I commit a lot of mistakes and am often reprimanded by my customers for that. But, such highly educated doctors, how could they do this…. (to my daughter)??"

her father asked as he broke down. I was at loss for words to console him. My hospital staff made quick arrangements as cancer, by that time, had spread to her spine also. Her chances of survival were only 1 out of

100. At the most, she might live for only another 2 to 3 years. But we wanted to do our best. We gave her chemotherapy and radiation. By the grace of God, our efforts succeeded. Her cancer cells were destroyed and her health also improved. But her blindness remained. We fixed artificial eyes, so that she would appear near normal.

As it was sensational news, the child received toys and gifts from all over the world. She was able to forget her anguish while playing with those toys. She and her father stayed in New York for about 3 to 4 weeks. After her treatment, they returned to Hyderabad.

Thus, with the episode of Nasreen Banu, the entire Telugu-speaking region came to know my name and the name of Memorial Sloan- Kettering Cancer Center. Thereafter, at the very mention of cancer, I was the first and only doctor the people from that area would think of. "Nori Dattatreyudu, the doctor the chief minister Dr. Chennareddy personally consulted," in fact was the memory that lingered in the minds of so many prominent citizens. It had become a routine practice, thereafter, for them to consult me by phone if they or any of their relatives suffered from cancer. Those who could afford it would come directly to MSK in New York for treatment.

Chapter 10
GOD BY MY SIDE HERO'S HERO

The great Telugu poet and devotee Ramadasu (Kancharla Gopanna) ecstatically sang, "The Taraka Rama chant was bestowed upon me as I wished," praising the benevolence of Lord Rama. Perhaps I was also bestowed with such a boon so that I could redeem my indebtedness to the Telugu clan and my motherland.

Nandamuri Taraka Rama Rao (popularly known as NTR) is a household name in every Telugu family. Both as a film hero and later as the Chief Minister of the combined state of Andhra Pradesh, he was very popular. Although his social films also did very well, his mythological movies, where he essayed the roles of Hindu Gods Lord Rama and Lord Krishna, mesmerized audiences. People used to worship him as a demi God.

NTR founded his political party, "Telugu Desham," on March 29, 1982, giving a clarion call for "Atma Gouravam (The Self-Esteem) of Telugus." This was sensational in many ways. His coming to power within nine months from the inception of the party and becoming the chief minister of the state, sweeping the election results like the wind, was historic. Also, as the chief minister he has left an everlasting impact on the hearts of the Telugu people with his welfare measures, including "1 kg rice for 1 rupee" (rice is a staple diet of Telugus).

The heroes of my younger days were NTR and ANR (Akkineni Nageswara Rao). I was also one of those audience members spellbound by their movies.

In my childhood, I had never dreamt of meeting them, moreover I had never imagined that my meeting NTR would lead me to accomplish a great task in my life. But, as I have already narrated, I used to see NTR at the house of my friend Vasireddy Chandrasekhar Prasad's father-in-law while I was completing my M.D. at Osmania University.

In 1984, while he was the chief minister, NTR learned that his wife Mrs. Basava Tarakam was diagnosed with cancer. She was his maternal cousin (sister-in-law). They had twelve children.

As per the advice of the doctors there, he brought her to the U.S. for treatment.

Bolla Bulli Ramaiah was an elected member of parliament from Eluru of Andhra Pradesh and was also a minister in the cabinet of the Union government of India. He recommended my name to NTR and advised him to take his wife to Memorial Sloan Kettering Cancer Center for the best treatment.

Bulli Ramaiah phoned me and briefed me regarding the situation. She was, initially, taken to some other hospital in the U.S., but then shifted to my hospital. It was not the first time I'd met her. While I was working on my M.D. in Hyderabad at Osmania University, I visited her house along with my friend Vasireddy Chandrasekhar Prasad and treated her for an infection.

When Mrs. Basava Tarakam came to the U.S for treatment, we treated her in our hospital first as an in-patient and then as an out-patient for the rest of the time. During those days, she used to visit my home. By the time she had come to the U.S., her cancer was in an advanced stage. But, despite that, the way she behaved was very dignified.

She used to lament, "Doctor! As I am the wife of a chief minister, I can come here for treatment, but how about the commoners from Andhra Pradesh?? Is there no way for them to obtain a qualitatively superior treatment?" The immediate question that followed in the same breath was, "Why don't you start a hospital there, Doctor?"

Although she posed that question very innocently, the motive behind that was indeed laudable. It triggered my thought process.

Can I alone start a cancer hospital? As a cancer specialist, I have the knowledge and the expertise. But is it a joke to think I could construct a hospital and manage it? ….. especially too with her high expectations for the treatment for cancer of the common people of Andhra Pradesh?? Why not? Was this not the ultimate motive and purpose of my lifelong endeavor?? Counter questions goaded my mind. Is my goal being realized through her? A multitude of thoughts swarmed my mind. But it was not a task that could be accomplished by a single man. Her wish became NTR's goal. Nothing can hinder it now.

unveiling the dedication stone which bears the names of Shri NTR myself, and Dr K Siva Prasad.

Shri NTR leading me to the venue.

Smt. Nandamuri Basava Taraka Rama Rao Memorial Cancer Foundation Trust

Cordially invites you to the function of laying Foundation Stone of the Hospital Complex

By

Dr. N.T. RAMA RAO
Hon'ble Chief Minister of Andhra Pradesh

at 9 a.m. on Sunday, the 16th July, 1989

SWAMI RANGANATHANANDA
has kindly consented to preside

Dr. P.B. DESAI
Director, Tata Memorial Hospital, Bombay

and

Dr. NORI DATTATREYA
Sloan Katering Memorial Hospital, New York

will be Guests of Honour

Venue: Road No. 14, Banjarahills, Near L.V. Prasad Eye Institute

Shri N. T. R was honoring me during the groundbreaking ceremony events of the Basavatarakam Indo American Cancer Institute Hyderabad.

NTR, who was visiting her, called for a meeting of non-resident Andhrites in Pittsburgh to attract investments. He sent word for me to meet him. Hence, I also went.

He welcomed me with great affinity.

Brimming with emotion and holding my hands, he said, "Basava Tarakam is my maternal cousin and my wife. She stood by me during the vicissitudes of life and has taken great care of me, my family, and my children, and has been sailing all of us very safely through our lives. I am ready to do anything for her. You shall save her."

As I had already examined her, I could reassure him of doing our best to help her. After a few months, in 1985, I learned that she had died in India. I felt very much pained.

As a doctor within the course of my duties, I come across many victims of cancer. If the patient responds well to the treatment, gets cured, and returns home, I feel good. But if the patient dies...... every death, every time, throws me into the pangs of anguish. The pain is worse if the victim is either a child or woman.... especially the death of any mother with her children surviving her.

When Mrs. Basava Tarakam died of cancer. She had children of different ages. Most of them were very young. That really bothered me a lot. Above all, in spite of her suffering from cancer herself, the way she thought of the commoners amazed me and inspired me to seriously think about her idea.

When I went to India, I met NTR on a courtesy call. He instantaneously initiated the "Nandamuri Basava Tarakam Memorial Cancer Foundation." Apart from me, he nominated Dr. Kakarla Subbarao, Dr. Kodela Siva Prasad, and Mr. Krishnam Raju as members of its board. He intended that the foundation, along with a few other organizations, should build a cancer hospital.

The state government allocated land for the hospital in the Banjara Hills of Hyderabad. But it was an uneven land full of stones and rocks!

In one week flat, the land was cleared and leveled, the roads were laid around it, and the "Shamianas" (a kind of decorative tents) were erected to perform the "foundation ceremony." When I set out for the ceremony, I went crazy to discover along the roads, my larger-than-life "cut outs," billboards depicting me! Normally, fans erect cut outs for their demi god - NTR, but NTR got them erected for me!!

On November 25, 1989 the foundation was laid for the hospital. He saw that I broke the ceremonial coconut (a Hindu ritual). I can never forget the speech he delivered on that occasion. "Many talented doctors like Dr. Nori Dattatreyudu are willing to serve the motherland and redeem their indebtedness. We shall utilize their services. I might be the hero for the Telugus, but he being a doctor relentlessly fighting with the dangerous cancer and saving the lives of many people, he is the "Real Hero!" Thus was his exciting rhetoric. I was on cloud nine!

After the completion of these rituals, he hosted a feast of "lunch" for some of us in his own residence at Abids in Hyderabad. He made me sit next to him. He didn't know that I was a pure vegetarian. He said jovially, "Doctor! I have got special prawns from Vizag (Visakhapatnam is a coastal town

in northern Andhra Pradesh)

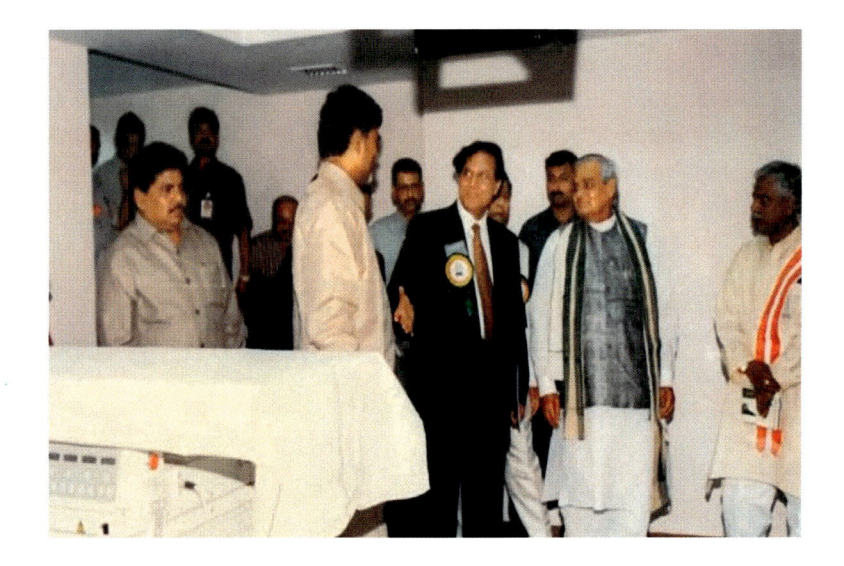

explaining the latest technology to the honorable Prime Minister and the Chief Minister.

especially for you." He also started serving me one dish after another, frequently prompting me to eat. I could not tell him the truth (that I am a pure vegetarian) but somehow managed to escape. NTR is himself a gourmet and enthusiastic in encouraging others also to eat well.

The next time that I visited Hyderabad, he invited me to the shooting of his new movie "Vishwamitra" (a Hindu sage). He had returned to shooting a movie while he was now acting as the chief minister of the state. Since he was an early riser, I also woke up at 4 am and set out to the shooting.

"Doctor! How would you feel attending the hospital after stopping your professional practice for 15 years?" He cracked a joke about himself, "My situation is the same as I left my acting career 15 years ago."

"Why do you say so, Sir? If you appear on the screen, that is enough.
Audiences will make it a super hit," I assured him.

This is not far from the truth. His stature was like that. Because he had stood by the hospital project, several people donated towards its construction. The construction was started. But when "Telugu Desham" (NTR's political party) lost the next election, it slowed down.

Every time I went to Hyderabad thereafter, Dr. Kakarla Subbarao, Dr. Kodela Siva Prasad, and I would meet. We used to deliberate as to how to take the project forward. I remember very well, one day in Irrum Manzil (an area in Hyderabad), while we were sipping tea in an Iranian restaurant (those are popular in Hyderabad), the same topic surfaced in our conversation.

"It is not moving forward. Whatever we do, there are no results," they opined. "Shall we stop now?" They spoke the truth. Whatever efforts we made, somehow it was not inching forward. A kind of despair and disappointment began overwhelming them.

But that day I was charged. I spoke with undaunted determination and self-confidence, "So far, whatever task I have undertaken, it never was left incomplete. Give me three months' time. Let us try."

Within myself I was also hurt. Perhaps that had triggered some kind of stubborn determination to somehow complete the hospital for the sake of cancer patients in India. Little did I know that this meeting

Addressing the audience regarding advances in cancer treatment in the U.S., and the mission and goals of Indo American Cancer Institute, Hyderabad.

would be a turning point and the pace setter for the establishment of one of the top five comprehensive cancer centers in India.

During that time, I went to deliver a lecture at a reputed hospital at Jerusalem in Israel called Hadassah Medical Center. It was a huge hospital. I enquired with its board members about its construction, maintenance, management, and resources, etc. What I heard amazed me! There is a women's organization in the U.S named Hadassah Women's Organization and it mobilizes the necessary resources for the hospital. Apart from amazement, I felt delighted also to know that.

If they could do it, so could we! A new confidence blossomed in me. After returning to New York, I met Dr. Polavarapu Tulasi Devi. She was from Kondoor village of Guntur district of Andhra Pradesh. She devotedly studied medicine and settled as a gynecologist in New York. Her husband Dr. Polavarapu Raghava Rao is an orthopedic surgeon. They came to the U.S earlier than my family and were very helpful to us. By orientation, they are service-minded.

I briefed Dr. Tulasi Devi about the way Hadassah Medical Center was being run.

Basava Tarakam Indo - American Cancer Institute Hyderabad, India

She also evinced interest. After our deliberations, we met with Dr. Gaddam Dasharatharami Reddy in his house. As a result of these deliberations, I started the American Telugu Women's Organization (ATWO). Dr. Tulasi Devi was the president. My wife Dr. Subhadra was the secretary. Dr. Gaddam Jyotsna Reddy was the treasurer.

All of us collectively organized a charity dinner. Women doctors and their husbands from different parts of the U.S. attended it and organized themselves into different branches to raise funds. They organized charity dinners and conducted several cultural programs and garnered funds.

With these funds reaching India, the construction of the hospital received an impetus. I named the hospital Indo-American Cancer Hospital and Research Center.

As was wished by Mrs. Nandamuri Basava Tarakam, the cancer hospital in her memory was started in Hyderabad. On June 22, 2000, it was opened by the then Prime Minister of India, Sri Atal Bihari Vajpayee.

However, just by donating the money, we still couldn't provide world-class cancer treatment facilities to the poor and needy, as she intended. Therefore, we the doctors in the U.S. resolved to transfer the skill set and the technology as well.

We also changed the name

My self and Mr. N. Balakrishna Chairman of the Board

My self and Mr. N. Balakrishna Chairman & Board Members

of American Telugu Women's Organization into the more broad-based Indo American Cancer Organization (IACO). As envisaged, we have passed on modern technology to Hyderabad. I have gotten the local staff trained by my expert U.S. teams. I have ensured that their knowledge is updated regularly. I also frequently visited the hospital myself to enable the local resources to learn the newest nuances in the domain.

Started as a 125-bed facility, it quickly crossed the 250-mark, and now it is a 750- bed hospital. Departments have been added: Apart from the hospital, a school of nursing, laboratories, post-graduate training in sub-specialties such as surgical oncology, radiation oncology, medical oncology, surgical pathology, etc., and a center for cancer research have been added. Now, it is a well-developed comprehensive cancer center with technology and a scope of services on par with the West.

I don't claim that it is my individual attainment, but collectively accomplished with the help of good Samaritans, service-minded people, citizen benefactors, doctors and the government.

Dr. Tulasi Devi Polavarapu died recently. It is a great loss to us, but her inspiration continues to be embodied in every non-resident Indian doctor. Like dedicated soldiers, all of us have been endeavoring 24/7 to provide all the resources in Hyderabad on par with those of the U.S.

With so much of a collective effort, world-class cancer care has become accessible and affordable to the ordinary people of the country. Within a short time, the Indo-American Cancer Hospital and Research Center has become one of the five top-ranking cancer hospitals of India and has earned international reputation too!

I am immensely happy I had a role in building such a hospital complex with advanced facilities for cancer treatment, education and training, and research.

I had witnessed, perhaps, the most pathetic situations in cancer care at the beginning of my medical career. For cancer care to rise from such a nadir to reach the current level, and to have been a steppingstone for such accomplishment, makes me happy. Others joining me and lending their support enhances the emotion.

If I have to consider my life-time achievements, I whole-heartedly claim that this is one of my top accomplishments.

Chapter 11

FOSTER DAUGHTER-FOSTER FATHER

Dr. Zvi Fuks studied medicine at Hebrew University in Jerusalem worked there for some years before coming to the U.S. He took over as the Chairman of the radiation department of Memorial Sloan-Kettering Cancer Center in 1984. He was well-known for cancer treatment and did much research in the subject. Somehow his taking over the department created a stir. The staff who had been working up until then started leaving the hospital and joined other institutions. Dr. Basil Hilaris had also left. He insisted on my joining him, but I did not leave MSK. Although, he caused an exodus, Dr. Fuks was very fond of me. He never interfered in my work and was very friendly with me.

In 1989, I was invited to take over as the Chairman of the oncology department at Booth Memorial hospital. In comparison with MSK, it was a small hospital. But I felt it was a challenge to develop it from the ground up into a comprehensive cancer center using my expertise and experience. I, therefore, decided to move. Dr. Fuks was not only unhappy with my decision but also opposed it. "Whatever you want I will get you here Dr. Datta, please stay here," was his repeated request. "All of my colleagues at MSK have agreed to support me."

But I convinced him that one gets this kind of opportunity only once in a blue moon and left for Booth Memorial Hospital in Queens, New York.

The Salvation Army is an international voluntary service organization belonging to the Protestant Christian Church. It has members all over the world. They are called the Salvationists. This organization is spread across 131 countries. Its objective is to help orphans, the poor, and the hungry. It was founded in 1865 in London by William and his wife Catherine Booth (nee Mumford).

The Salvation Army started a chain of hospitals in the U.S. and other countries in memory of its founder William Booth. All of those are called Booth hospitals after him. Thus, was started the

Booth Memorial and Medical Center in 1892 by the Salvation Army in the Manhattan area of New York. After 1957, it was shifted and developed in Queens.

It was a small hospital when I joined it. It was being run by voluntary service organization and had its innate financial problems.

Mr. Ned Arnold with my family, left to right:
my son Sateesh myself, my wife and my daughter Priya.

That was a big challenge for me.* Perhaps, the best consolation was that Booth Memorial was developing a relationship with both MSK and Cornell University. That
was a plus for me.

The skills, expertise, and the administrative efficiency I had acquired at those places became handy to prop my resolve to improve Booth Memorial Hospital. Therefore, I embarked on a multi-purpose project. As a first step, I raised funds from a few wealthy people, charities, and other organizations to buy modern equipment, tools to update the infrastructure.

Unless a hospital gains a good reputation of excellent treatment and ultra-modern facilities, patients don't throng to it. But as I envisioned, the reputation and consequently the number of patients has increased. When I joined, there were only two more doctors in my department of

Radiation-oncology and hence, to meet the increased demand, I

with Mr. Ned Arnold, my American father and Pamela Dawson his daughter.

had had to recruit more and more doctors. Thus, I continued to expand the department.

If the cancer patients who are cured of or gained relief from it could share their experiences, it would not only inspire others but also provide a reasonable understanding of cancer treatment and its success. With this thought, I initiated there a program called "Celebration of Life." During this celebration, patients I had treated came from all over the world and shared their experiences. We captured their presentations on video and distributed them to others. The "Celebration" has really given a great fillip to the popularity and growth of the hospital.

We also published a monthly newsletter highlighting the various initiatives and developmental activities of the hospital. The newsletter was sent to all reputed American universities. That garnered a lot of attention for our hospital. At the same time, we rolled out certain attractive programs to interest more students too. One of them was a four-year post-graduate residency program for medical graduates. New and innovative ideas always imbue fresh impetus!

We also started a 2-year fellowship program as a next step. We ensured that we attracted great talent from all over the world to join our residency and fellowship programs. Within 2 to 3 years, we reached a stage when bright minds started competing to get admission into our programs. Leveraging my relationships with professionals from the domain, we started inviting renowned doctors, erudite professors, and reputed researchers to visit our hospital, and organized their lectures on pertinent topics.

As I claimed earlier, I am not only an expert in Brachytherapy using the computer but also a researcher. If the hard-earned results of my knowledge were to reach the patients, medical students, and doctors of the next generation, there needed to be a Brachytherapy center there. Hence, slowly I raised funds and established a Brachytherapy center at Booth Memorial Hospital. From another 2 or 3 doctor colleagues when I joined it, Booth Memorial was able to quickly progress within 3 or 4 years to be a super specialty hospital with over 150 oncologists.

To put it succinctly, in 4 to 5 years, from a small hospital with limited facilities, I developed Booth into a highly reputed, large and comprehensive cancer center. That gave me immense satisfaction. To put it in one phrase, the hospital was like my "foster daughter."

Whatsoever was my hard work and endeavor, if I claim that I had done it singlehandedly, it would not be correct because if I do not talk about a person who stood by me like a rock -- nay...like a father -- my success story would not be complete. His name was Ned Arnold.

When I joined Booth Memorial, Ned Arnold was an honorary trustee on the hospital board of trustees. As a benefactor of that area, he always used to contemplate doing something good for the people there. He used to share his ideas with me. In the process, we became good friends. Our relationship had become so strong, he was known among my friends as my "American foster father."

He had a very interesting background. He was born on Nov 27, 1906 in Brooklyn. His father was a mechanic. He started to develop an interest in business and auto-motive services from the early age of 14 while assisting his father as a helper in the garage. Later, on his own, he started a business venture called "The Tire

Distributing Corporation"

With Ms. Natalie Masino my administrator for over 30 years

when he was hardly 20 years. It earned a great reputation. Arnold's knowledge and business acumen in the truck maintenance business earned him international repute. That's why the then U.S. president Dwight D. Eisenhower made him a member of the "Conference on Highway Safety" as well as city and state councils of highway safety. Thus, he also had a good relationship with the White House.

He was the president of the Queens Chamber of Commerce for several terms. In addition, he was the director of the State Chamber of Commerce. He was the Chairman of the Greater New York Red Cross Society too. He used to like flight voyages. He, therefore, started the "Long Island Flying Service." In 1970, a huge fire accident gutted his entire business. By that time, Arnold was 65. However, he never despaired, but rebuilt his business empire again. The journey of his life inspired me a great deal.

Asians have a few misgivings about the familial and matrimonial relationships of the west. But those are not justified. Take Arnold only as an example: He fell in love with and married Julia when he was young. Their marriage lasted for 68 years.

Thereafter, he was alone. Most of my acquaintances and friends are like that and have had a good life. Pamela Arnold, daughter of Julia and Ned Arnold, was like my sister. Her husband, Arthur Dawson, was also a good friend of mine. In fact, they were like my family.

Mr. Arnold was discussing his proposal for a significant donation to the hospital on my behalf, which subsequently created the Ned Arnold Center for oncology at NYP Queens Hospital for which I became the first Director.

Arnold and I used to talk to each other quite often. We used to narrate the stories of our childhood. Both of us, although we cannot claim to be poor, did struggle a lot early to come up in life. Surprisingly, both of us shared a common habit of carrying with us a pack of cash. Perhaps the habit used to give us lots of confidence and courage. This was a common trait in both of us. During our lunch hour or in the evening, we used to bet to guess how much cash each one of us was carrying and have a hearty laugh while verifying it.

He used to share a lot of anecdotes, during those times. In the 1940s and 50s, several times the American stock markets crashed. Some of the wealthy people who suffered heavy losses due to a crash could not bear the shock. Hence, they would jump from high-rise buildings in despair.

"Datta! Those days, I never used to understand why they

committed suicide. I did not have money at that time. Unless you have money and lose it, how would you know the pain of losing it? Now I know," Arnold used to say laughingly.

Many people used to come to him for donations. He never used to refuse anybody. If somebody asked for 5 thousand, he might give at the most 2 thousand. He carried a great reputation as a donor in Queens. Whenever, he visited my home, he used to give lavish gifts to my children.

He was of great support to me to expand the hospital. Wherever possible, he liked to push my name to prominence. If my department grew from 2,000 sq. ft. to 25,000 sq. ft., it was not only my hard work but his meticulous planning that helped it. He used to back me to the hilt for the annual program of "Celebration of Life," not only in raising funds, but also in deliberating about every decision and then being a great supporter thereof.

In 1992, New York Hospital took over Booth Hospital from the Salvation Army and the name was changed to New York Hospital Queens. Ned Arnold became its trustee for life. The Arnold couple donated a huge amount to the hospital.

Acknowledging it with gratitude, I insisted and got the radiation oncology department renamed as the "Julia and Ned R. Arnold Center." Ned Arnold lived his life to the fullest independently and died at the age of 94. Although I don't remember the sorrow for the loss of my father as I lost him at my early age, when Arnold passed away, I could certainly feel it. No words can express my personal loss and, for me, no one can replace him.

Chapter 12

HUMBLY HONING THE SKILLS

Booth Memorial Hospital Queens had an affiliation with Memorial Sloan-Kettering Cancer Center, Cornell Medical College, and Cornell University. Hence, my relationship with those organizations also continued. Those organizations used to come to know what I was doing at Booth's either through the newsletter or through other doctors and professors. In 1990, I also started working as a professor of clinical radiology-radiation oncology at Cornell Medical College of New York Hospital.

Impressed by the rapid progress at Booth, especially the research and clinical programs I had introduced, the president and CEO of New York Hospital, Dr. David Skinner, bought Booth in 1992 and combined it with Cornell Medical Center.

His full name was David Barnard Skinner. We used to call him Dr. Skinner. Born in 1935, he came out of Yale Medical School with flying colors. He acquired expertise both in general and thoracic surgeries.

with Dr Zvi Fuks in Israel. He was my chairman at MSKCC New York. He was also the Director of Hadassah Medical Center in Jerusalem.

With my mentor Dr Ted Beattie chief of Memorial Sloan Kettering with another Chairman.

So much so, when he was chief resident and teaching fellow at Harvard Medical School, he was praised as "King of the East." Later, he joined the renowned John Hopkins Medical School and became an expert in esophageal ailments, including cancer. Even the most complicated cases that other doctors refused to treat; he used to take up. It is not easy to wear three hats -- of a surgeon, a scientist, and a teacher simultaneously-- and yet earn a great repute.

With the same sincerity with which he worked and with the same intense enthusiasm, he used to encourage his juniors and savor their success. That's how his students were eventually able to occupy high posts in almost all hospitals in the U.S. After 15 years at the University of Chicago, in 1987 he joined Cornell Medical Center of New York Hospital as President-CEO. The medical center had been incurring losses at the time he took over, which he estimated as one million U.S. dollars per week.

It was a big challenge to the executive in him to turn the losses into profit with multi-pronged strategies. Later, he relentlessly worked to establish a huge network. He almost immersed himself in that task

with my colleagues from MSKCC. L-R me, Dr Zelefsky, Dr Hilaris, Dr Harrison (represent four Chiefs of service at MSKCC in 75 years) who shaped the treatment of cancer with brachytherapy in the world.

throughout his life. But, interestingly, however busy he was in his administrative work, he never relegated the diligent surgeon in him to a less important role.

In 1997, both New York Hospital and Columbia Presbyterian Hospital merged into one and became the biggest academic medical center in the whole of the U.S. The merger was overseen solely by Dr. Skinner. Dr. Skinner was its CEO-President. That network has over 32 hospitals in it. The entire credit goes to him alone. Quite often, Dr. Skinner would say, "We shall dream big and to attain these dreams we shall take the entire team forward."

Under his guidance Booth Memorial Hospital was purchased by New York Hospital and was renamed as "The New York Hospital Medical Center of Queens." That's how I encountered Dr. Skinner.

U.S. Secretary of Health and Human Services Dr. L Sullivan recognizing me in a national conference for my contributions to medicine in the U.S.

Speaking very highly of me to everybody, Dr. Skinner would often say, "Dr. Nori's caliber and determination played a very important role in transforming a small hospital into a multi-specialty hospital. In fact, because of his presence, we paid the premium amount to buy that hospital."

In 1993, another innovation I had made was to connect all my departments in the network of 18 institutions with a central computer networking system. This was a pioneering task executed in the U.S. for the very first time. When Dr. Skinner visited my department, I could show him the waiting time of the patients from other network hospitals and the measures taken to reduce it. That was the first time he participated in the centralized computer networking system, and he liked it immensely. Thereafter, he introduced it in all the hospitals under him.

"I am appointing Dr. Nori as the chairman of the department," announced Dr. Skinner and made me so. In the normal course, there was a selection committee. If they searched by advertisement, doctors could apply. Then, there would be two to three rounds of elimination and thereafter two more rounds of interviews, followed by deliberations,

During the inauguration of the Cancer Center by me in São Paulo Brazil in 1987.

reports, etc. It was a long-drawn-out process. It might take two years for the whole process to be completed.

Brushing aside all those formalities, in one sentence, he had announced me as the chairman of the department! He was so powerful, no one dared to question him.

Because of the agreement between both of those hospitals, while continuing to be the Director of the Cancer Center, I had to take up the mantle of the chairmanship of the Radiation Oncology Department at New York Hospital Queens as well as at Cornell Medical Center in Manhattan. These combined departments constituted one of the largest oncology departments in the U.S.

At the peak of my career, I was simultaneously holding three major leadership positions

As a director of major cancer centers and Chairman of two academic radiation oncology departments.

Then onwards for 20 years my relentless journey has been very successful.

Group of doctors from various countries (UK,USA, Japan, South America, Argentina, France, and Italy) attended a meeting in London chaired by me on behalf of IAEA, International atomic energy agency

Immersing myself in the research of Brachytherapy, I was able to unveil new regimes of treatment that made qualitatively superior treatment for various types of cancers affordable. I was able to create treatments that could control cancer in a highly reduced span of treatment time, with lesser expenses, and in a less painful way.

One bright light can light ten more lights. It shall, indeed. One fruit tree helps Nature for ten more to germinate. It is not that I alone shall grow but shall help those around me also to grow. Then only are we human. This has been my philosophy/conviction.

Therefore, from among my colleagues, I selected those who were interested, and trained them in Brachytherapy to be as good as I am. If there were five Brachytherapy Centers in the U.S, three were under my guidance and leadership. With those who were working there, I could sincerely share my knowledge. Through them, the fruition of that sharing reached many a patient.

As a university professor, I could mold my students as expert doctors. Most of them are now working as radiation oncologists across the world. Many of them were able to grow and became directors of some of the biggest academic departments. In any country of the world, chances are that one will find, at the least, one of my students. These accomplishments make me very happy.

In any field, if we neglect the fast-paced developments and do not suitably and continuously upgrade our skills, we become stagnant. That's why, whatever research I have conducted and new observations I have made, I have documented and shared that know-how with other medical professors and students whenever I visited their universities on their invitation.

I was also on many national and international committees as a member. At times, I served as secretary or president of some of them.

I was invited as a visiting professor to deliver lectures on advances on Cancer to various academic centers and Universities around the globe include Russia, China, Germany, U.K., France, Canada, South Africa, South America, Argentina, Australia, New Zealand and Israel.

My Awards and Recognitions

1) Consultant to the United Nations International Atomic Energy Agency (IAEA), advising in the formulation of guidelines for cancer treatment in developing countries.

2) Chief Scientific Advisor to Pravara Institute of Medical Sciences, a 1,000 bed multi-specialty hospital in Loni, Maharashtra.

3) Chief Patron and Chief Scientific Advisor to Dr. Vithal Rao Vikhe Patil Foundation Comprehensive Cancer Center, Ahmadnagar, Maharashtra.

4) The most prestigious "Tribute to Life" Award presented by the American Cancer Society.

5) Most Distinguished Physician Award" presented by Memorial Sloan-Kettering Cancer Center.

6) The Nargis Dutt Memorial Foundation in the U.S. and the network of Indian Professionals in the U.S. honored me with the "Excelsior Award".

7) The American Association of Physicians of Indian Origin (AAPI) honored me with the "Most Distinguished Physician Award".

8) In 2014, received the highest civilian award in the U.S. "The Ellis Island Medical of Honor" for exemplary and outstanding qualities in both personal and professional life.

9) Recognized as one of the Top Doctors for Cancer in the U.S. and Top Doctor for Women's Cancer in the U.S. for over two decades by his peers of 100,000 oncologists.

10) The Indian Medical Association honored me with a Gold Medal for providing advanced training in the
U.S. for Indian Physicians.

11) The government of India recognized my contributions to medicine with the "Padma Shri" Award in 2015.

12) In 2016, The Sankriti Organization honored me with "Bharat Gaurav Award" at the British Parliament in London.

13) In 2016, Krishna University and Sri Venkateswara University in Andhra Pradesh honored me with Doctorate degrees.

14) In December 2017, the 10,000 member oncologists of the Indian Cancer Congress honored me with their highest recognition "Living Legend in Cancer" award for my contributions to cancer care in India, the U.S. and around the globe.

15) In 2021, I am appointed as an Advisor to Government of Andhra Pradesh to streamline the comprehensive cancer services in that state.

16) Recognized with Fellow status by the American College of Radiology.

17) Recognized with Fellow status by the American Society of Therapeutic Radiology and Oncology.

18) Recognized with Fellow status by the American College of Radiation Oncology.

19) President of the New York Cancer Society.

20) President of the American Brachytherapy Society.

Chapter 13

DIVINE ORDINANCE ETCHED IN STONE

In the U.S., I have not faced any discrimination on the grounds of color, appearance, or nationality. I tried to observe their culture, practices, and habits and imbibed the good values and traditions as I believe we must emulate the good wherever it is. I don't want anybody to point an accusing finger towards me. That's why I have been always very, very careful and preferred to sincerely learn more than the locals and relentlessly work harder than they. By nature, I believe in being good and practice it too. Neither do I go by any stubborn dogma.

My colleague friends and presidents of the hospitals often jocularly remark, "Dr. Nori kills us by his good nature."

Mostly because of my parents, the way they brought me up, and being from a big joint family of many siblings, I must have been imbued with that kind of nature and courteousness. Although sometimes I may have become angry with some people or about certain circumstances, it has never been intense. I read somewhere, "Anger is like cinders in our hands, even before we throw it upon somebody else it burns us." How true!! Therefore, I don't carry anger too long; it is not my nature.

This attitude has helped me a lot. Not only my equals, but also those above me in the hierarchy, were always courteous and affectionate towards me. Encouraging me from teaching to research, they stood by me. Although my co-doctors, other staff, and patients hail from diverse countries with diverse backgrounds, I have been able to seamlessly mingle with them.

Nevertheless, however good we are, there might be people unjustifiably jealous of us. I also faced such incidents once or twice in my life. There had been one or two characters that had been waiting to catch me on a wrong foot. An Israeli youth worked as a fellow with me. We jointly authored a paper. After his returning to his country, he authored another paper using some material from our joint work. Perhaps he made a mistake.

Taking advantage of the situation, people there raised a storm accusing me of committing a blunder. "We should also reassess all the papers Dr. Nori has published in the past," they insisted. Hence, the hospital appointed a committee to go through my papers. There were about 300 scientific publications. The committee closely perused and examined all of them repeatedly. It took almost two years, and they could not find an iota of wrongdoing. I maintained a measured silence with patience, all through.

Finally, the committee totally exonerated me, attributing whatever mistakes only to the Israeli doctor and confirming that I didn't have any role in such misfeasance. I emerged unscathed and blemish free.

I always firmly believe, both by word and deed, that only hard work, quality and sincerity would take one to places. I have practiced what I believed. For me, respect is more important than money.

I am not a "glass is half empty" pessimist, but a strong "glass is half full" optimist. I always keep a distance from naysayers. I believe that if our intent is good, God also dispenses blessings favorably. I like those people who work with a conviction to make the glass full. If anything is achieved in the world, it is made possible only by them.

The origin of all my strong convictions lies in the spirituality and the devotion to the God almighty that I have inherited from my parents. Spirituality and daily life were not separate for them but seamlessly merged into one. I see God in every act. I inherited this belief from them.

Every morning before I set out to my work, I pray to the supreme divinity. I urge him to equip me with the Caliber to examine and treat my patients with the appropriate remedy and the patients with the ability to quickly recover from their ailment and return home. I firmly believe that beyond medicine and science, there is a force which is Supreme, and we call it God. That's why I never leave home without offering my prayers to God. My wife Subhadra also knows by heart the prayer of the Sun, " Aditya Hrudayam." The Sun as the source of good health is a faith for ages.

I resolved to initiate a few good things in memory of my late parents. As a first step, in 1998, Subhadra and I started a charitable trust named "Nori Foundation." The objective was to provide education and medical aid to the needy as well as other services to society. In

Shirdi Sai Baba Mandir in New Jersey established by Nori Foundation

the process, the idea to construct a temple in the U.S. to Shirdi Shirdi Saibaba (an Indian holy man who has now been deified).

I have been a strong devotee of Shirdi Saibaba from my medical college days at Kurnool. Whenever I spent some time in the precincts of Sai temple on the banks of River Tungabhadra, I used to feel reinvigorated by some great force. There is no doubt about Shirdi Sai's divinity. He was not limited to a few holy chants and miracles but was a humanist. He resented blind faith. He paved the way of life beyond, or transcending, castes and religions. He led a simple life where he could witness God in every living being – be it human, be it an animal. Anybody in the world can easily follow his philosophy and aphorisms.

I wanted to disseminate that philosophy of universal love and religious harmony in the West also. Perhaps God was willing! It is not an easy endeavor to construct a temple in the U.S. There are many rules and restrictions. Temples can be built only in the specific zones earmarked for prayer halls. Apart from other regulations, parking space is one of the conditions.

I needed such a place nearby New York, but one was not available however hard we had tried. One morning on a Thursday (or "Guru varam," which was meant to be dedicated to "Gurus," the teachers), in my mind, I had had a quarrel with the God: "Today is the last day: If you can't show me a suitable place today, I may shelve the very idea of constructing a temple for you." It was a childlike internal squabbling.

Meanwhile, a patient who had been treated 15 years ago came for a routine check-up that day. As a final resort, I inquired of her, "What do you do?"

Surprise! Surprise!!

"I am in the real estate business, Doctor! If you need anything, kindly tell me," she answered me.

I silently thanked the God and told her that I was looking for a place with adequate parking for a temple in an appropriate zone.

"The moment I reach my office from here, I will search, find out, and tell you about the availability of that kind of place," she assured me. As promised, she found a property and also fixed an appointment with the seller. The same day, I went and made an agreement to buy it!

at the Shirdi Sai Mandir, New Jersey
annual celebration conducted at the Royal Albert Palace.

This was in the year 2001, and so the construction of the temple started.

When I went to India, my aunt and uncle took me to a Baba temple at Punjagutta, in Hyderabad and introduced me to a retired professor who was supervising the activities of the temple there. He offered to help me in my temple construction work.

The sculptors' family who made the statue at Shirdi in India made a statue of about 6 ft. tall, 4 ft. wide and weighing about 3 tons for my temple. Pembarti sculptors made ornamental accessories such as a crocodile banner, a silver throne, carvings for the canopy, and lions very similar to those of the Shirdi temple. The statue of Baba arrived in the U.S.

The professor and the so-called "Guru" from Hyderabad came to the U.S. for the inauguration of the "Mandir" (Temple). I don't know what had corrupted his mind. In a few months, he filed a case against me in the U.S., claiming that the U.S. temple belonged to him and demanded a whopping 50 million U.S. dollars from me as compensation. The case went on for 6 months and after listening to the arguments from both sides, the court with 12 jurors gave a unanimous verdict favorable to

Devotees at our Shirdi Sai Baba Mandir in Long Island, New York

me. Also, he was barred from entering the U.S. It is not out of place to mention that upon specific inquiry by the presiding judge about the unanimity of the jurors on the verdict, they answered that they could not find an iota of culpability from a person of Dr. Nori's stature.

During those six months, severe despair and depression had taken over me. Several questions used to plague me, such as "Why all these problems when I endeavored to do something good?" "Would I fail to pay back the loan and the down payment on time?" But every time I began to despair, I was able to obtain a timely resolution and solace.

Everybody faces a test sometime in life. This may goad us. God tests our caliber and also brings out our fullest potential. He equips us to shoulder the tasks that we believe are beyond our capacity. This was what I realized as I was going through the tough times.

Surpassing all stumbling blocks, construction of Sai temple was completed. On July 4, 2002, the process of divine installation was completed.

Thereafter, I was able to get one more chance to build a temple again. Nay, the chance was given by Sainath alone. In 2008 I constructed one more temple in Iselin in the state of New Jersey. It was named Shirdi Sai Cultural and Community Center.

In both above temples, separate abodes have been carved for Lord Ganesh, Nav Grahas (Nine Planets) and Goddess Lakshmi. Eight traditional Vedic scholars ("Pundits") from India came to the U.S. and conducted daily "Pooja" (worship) and rituals in the most religious way. They meticulously follow the same procedure of worship, rituals, and insulation in divine light ("Aarati") as is being done at Shirdi in India. In 2019, I established the third Sai Mandir in Hicksville, Long Island, New York.

The objective of these three temples is to disseminate the values that Sainath preached and the sincerity and patience he practiced. They always inspire me to further progress in the path of service. However hard I toil, the moment I go to any of those temples the tranquility prevailing there gives me huge relief.

They do not have any board or board of directors. They simply follow the ordinance of Sainath. These two "Mandirs" (temples) are not limited only to worship and any religious vows but also have become centers of culture. They run programs called "Bala Vikas" to inculcate good values in children. They also teach Indian traditional music and classical dances. To learn these in the U.S., students from 3 years old to 15 years throng here. Teachers have voluntarily joined and taken up that responsibility.

Over the last 20 years, many Swamijis and orators of religious discourse have visited the temples. They blessed the devotees with their religious preaching. Many a singer came and worshipped ''Sai'' with their rendering of divine nectar. Pandit Jasraj spent hours together and sang in ecstasy in the divine presence of the lord.

I can't claim that this was done solely by me or that I alone constructed those temples. I was only a tool to spread the good deeds of Saibaba through those temples. When so many challenges and stumbling blocks stared in my face, the fact that I was still able to overcome them only strengthened and increased my belief in Baba.

I would like to acknowledge with my sincere thanks the continued support of Sri Pailla Malla Reddy and his wife

Devotees at our Shirdi Sai Baba Mandir in New Jersey

Sardhana Garu, Sri Anumolu Subba Rao and his wire Rajeswari Garu, Amit and Veena Shah, Kanak and Prabha Golia and Dr. and Mrs. Tarun Wasil.

At this juncture, I have to recollect those dedicated devotees of Baba who unfailingly and unconditionally helped me in the construction of the temples: Vijaya Malladi, Nori Balasubramanyam and Anatha, Nori Girish and Anuradha, Tadepalli Ramesh and Sharada, Nori Vasanta, Kalluri Sujata and Gopal, Pendyala Chandu and Suma, Neppalli Venku, Yamijala Kalyan and Janaki, Neppalli Prasad Rao and Lakshmi, Nanduri Annapoorna and Sudhakar, Murali Kajur, Nori Srinivas and Arundhati, Lanka Kutumba Rao and Rani, Lanka Ramanand and Kalyani, and Kiran and Vinod Motwani and Pryia Pisipati. They always stood by me during that time and continue to do so even now.

Nori Foundation cherishes these goals: to enhance human values, harmoniously bridge diverse cultures, and strive for good in unity.

Chapter 14

BACK TO THE FUTURE

After the Padma awards ceremony, Mr. K.P. Singh organized a party for us at his home. Thereafter, for about two hours, members of the press swarmed around me. In the evening, The Delhi Telugu Association honored me in a big way. After this, the congress party leader, the then parliamentarian and businessman Mr. T. Subbarami Reddy organized a get-together, or shall I say celebration? The reputation he carries is that whatever he does, he does it mighty large. Matching his reputation, political bigwigs like Digvijay Singh, Gulam Nabi Azad, and several Bollywood celebrities, including Mrs. Sharmila Tagore, attended. My God-sister, Sridevi, along with her family, flew down to Delhi to attend

Function in New Delhi with Shri T SubbiRami Reddy, Sridevi and Smt. Sharmila Tagore another legendary Bollywood actress.

the celebration. It was as grand as the Padma awards ceremony. It was such a beautiful day, and I will never forget it in my lifetime.

Later, I visited my home state Andhra Pradesh and shared my joy with my brothers, sisters, friends, and relatives.

They showered me with their compliments. I may feel happy about the recognition of my work, but I can never be complacent about my work.

Before I was conferred with Padmashri, I was also conferred with many significant and prestigious awards in America such as "Tribute to Life," "Distinguished Physician" and "Top Doctor for Cancer," etc. I believe these are all part of the recognition of my work.

In the state of Andhra Pradesh, the government has included a chapter on my biography in the curriculum for the students of the 9th standard in their textbook of Telugu. One of my nieces is a teacher in Tenali (a town in the state of Andhra Pradesh).

Exhilarated, she says, whenever she meets me, "I feel very proud while teaching that lesson to my students. With a lot of pride, I tell my students that you are my uncle!" I also feel happy about her feelings.

In 2016, both Sri Venkateshwara University and the Krishna University honored me by conferring honorary doctorates on me. Krishna University conducted my felicitation and the graduation ceremony in the very college where I had studied in Machilipatnam. I went around the college and the classrooms, feeling nostalgic and recollecting my aspirations and dreams in those younger days of becoming a doctor.

Such things overwhelm my heart. I am a winner – both at home and in the international arena.

Legendary actor Shri Akkineni Nageswara Rao (ANR), Dr C Narayana Reddy Garu, Dr T SubbiRami Reddy Garu honoring me for my contributions to medicine at the Ravindra Bharathi in Hyderabad

Shri ANR was presenting me with a "Suvarna Kankanam."

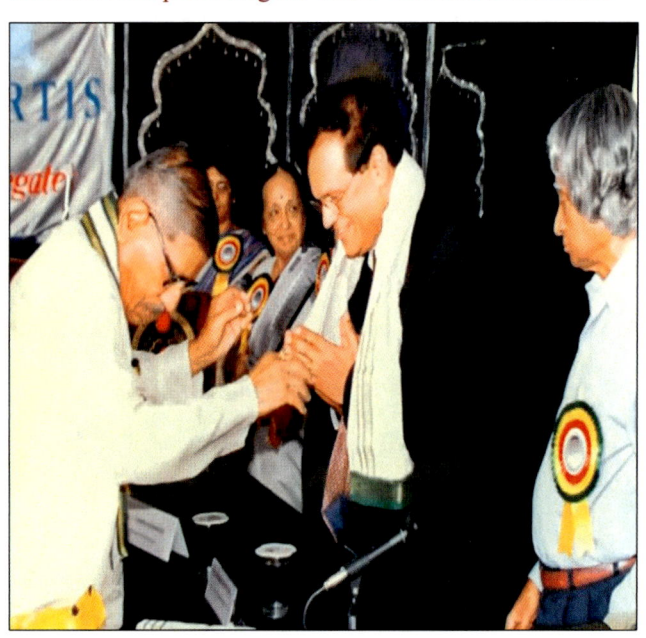

Sri Pulla Reddy was honoring me at
one of the medical meetings in Hyderabad.

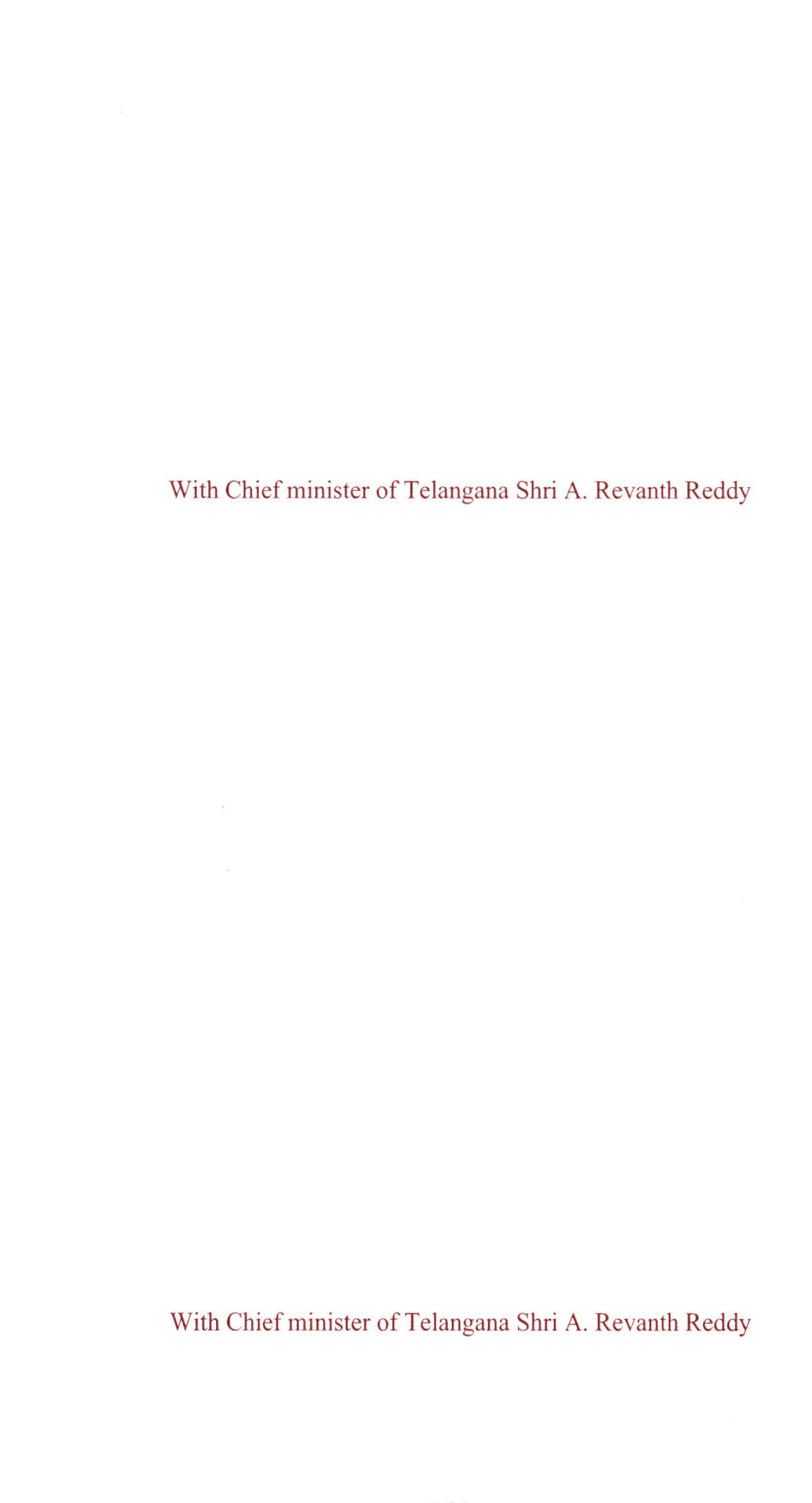

With Chief minister of Telangana Shri A. Revanth Reddy

With Chief minister of Telangana Shri A. Revanth Reddy

With our past President honorable Shri Abdul Kalam at an international meeting in Hyderabad organized by our Indo-American Cancer Institute.

Shri V Radhakrishna Patil was appointing me as the chief patron of Dr V. Patil foundation, a medical and educational institute complex at Ahmednagar Shirdi Maharashtra.

with Dr. C. Pratap Reddy Apollo Group of Hospitals

wWth my teacher and mentor
Dr Kakarla Subbarao at a function in Hyderabad.

With Dr B. Parthasaradhi Reddy, Chairman of Hetero group of companies

with legendary Shri S.P. Balasubramanian during my visit to his residence in 2019.

Dr. Karan Singh honoring me for his contributions to improve cancer care in India at the annual function of Indian national overseas Congress (I) in New York2013 Also seen Mr. Shudh Parkash Singh, President, INOC and Mr. George, Chairman of the Board, Inoc

Chapter 15

ON THE HOME TURF

My father-in-law and mother-in-law
Sri Tadepalli Srinivasa Rao and Smt. Savitri

Here, I must tell you something about my marriage.

Those days, in India, if a family were to give a daughter in marriage, apart from the bridegroom's character, his assets were of prime importance. Had the groom good property, he could get a good amount of dowry also. In that time, providing a dowry was very typical.

I belonged to a good family. I was also good, handsome, and intelligent. I had already completed my graduate degree in medicine. These were all my positive points.

I had lost my father at a young age. But for my good education,

I did not have any property or great status. These were my negative points. I did not have any familial obligations to sisters of marriageable age nor to younger brothers to be educated. That was another positive point.

with my family son, daughter, son-in-law, daughter-in-law, my grandkids. L-R is sitting Indu Nagar Prana Maheshwari, Jhansi Estella, Shaan Kumar, myself and my wife. Standing row: Priya, Abhinaya, Himanshu, Sateesh, and Joy.

But until that time, my brothers had taken care of me and provided for my education. I didn't have my own house, etc. These were other points on the negative side. Therefore, it was a little difficult to obtain a good marriage alliance for me.

Mr. Tadepalli Srinivasa Rao, who was a practicing Chartered Accountant at Nizamabad (a district headquarters in Telangana in the then combined state of Andhra Pradesh) evaluated all those pros and cons and yet decided to give his daughter Subhadra to me in marriage. Although he was rich, he did not want to give any dowry as a matter of principle. I was a rare bridegroom who accepted all those conditions. In fact, I never bothered about a dowry. My mother, my sisters, and other womenfolk also did not expect any customary gifts from the bride's family. So, her family liked me. My elder brother requested that they pay Rs.4000- (about $60 U.S.) towards marriage expenses. They settled for Rs.3500- (about $50 U.S.)!

with my brothers-in-law and their families at Priya's wedding. Left to right Arun Tadepalli, myself, Alekhya Tadepalli, Aditya Tadepalli, my wife, Suresh Tadepalli, Priya and Smt. Savitri Tadepalli Himanshu Nagar, Ashwin Tadepalli, Sharada Tadepalli.

My marriage with Subhadra was solemnized according to the Hindu customs on March 9, 1974 at Nizamabad.

Some of my cousins in the U.S often tease my wife by asking her, "You could get Dattu for $50 U.S.? Now we will pay you $30 million U.S. Return our Dattu to us."

My wife also takes it sportingly and makes a repartee with a smile, "No, no. Thirty million is not adequate. Increase the rate, I may then consider."

By the time of our marriage, Subhadra had also completed her degree in medicine (M.B.B.S) at Osmania College at Hyderabad. After our wedding, we started our life at a rented house in Nallakunta in Hyderabad.

I started working hard for the maintenance of the family. I had a good friend Yarramilli Krishna Rao from my Kurnool College days. His family had an alkali metal factory in the Uppal area of Hyderabad. Because of my acquaintance with him, I used to visit the factory as a consulting doctor 2 or 3 times a week. They paid me Rs.200- ($3 U.S.) per month.

My Daughter Priya Nori at her sweet 16 function

With my in laws and family

    I also opened a clinic in Nallakunta. Whenever I would not go to Uppal, I used to attend the clinic in the evenings. Patients normally prefer to go to a busy clinic. So, to give such a semblance, my second elder brother, his wife and children used to come and sit in the clinic. Thanks to their good intention and strategy, I had a good practice there. I also started issuing leave certificates on medical grounds to state and central government employees. By now, I was able to overcome my monetary problems.

On September 28, 1975, we had our first child, a boy, whom we named Sateesh.

Progress in their careers, research, etc. cause some professionals to neglect their families. But I am not one among them. I believe that family, near and dear ones, are very important for everyone. My conviction, from the beginning, has been that regarding one's spouse, children, parents, relatives and friends, one has to take great care of them, do whatever one can do for them, and share love with them. And this I meticulously practiced. Nothing can compensate for the loss of one's father. Losing my father, the guiding spirit, in my early childhood, compounded by

Bharata Natya Arangetram

Priya Nori
December 3, 1995

my daughter Priya learned Bharatanatyam since a very young age from a renowned dancer Srimati Kamala Laxman, Performing her Arangetram in 1995.

financial problems, are the early chapters of my life. I was to accept my fate. I am grateful to my maternal aunty (my mother's sister) Mrs., Jonnalagadda Sundaramma, but for whose help I could not have continued my education, thus surmounting my increasing monetary problems. My mother had also toiled very hard for me until I settled down in the U.S. Tears well up in my eyes at that very thought.

When I first settled in the U.S., it was a very hectic part of my life, both personally and professionally. It was also a period of my rapid progress, a very satisfying phase indeed. Initially, we bought a house on the banks of the Hudson River. After a few years, we built our own spacious house consisting of all the amenities, including a swimming pool and garden.

On one occasion, we conducted a board meeting of the Indo-American Cancer Hospital. That time Mr. G. Pulla Reddy, owner of the renowned sweet stall chain, G. Pulla Reddy Sweets, visited my house and after I showed him around it, he said, "Doctor! Many may not like it if we construct and live in a very big house. Be cautious."

He being a very experienced veteran of life lessons, I could not brush aside his comments. But, in a way, my construction of that house epitomized my perceived success after my childhood poverty. Pulla Reddy, in spite of his lofty status in the society, was very humble. Although he was extremely wealthy, he lived in a humble abode. Yet he had constructed a huge "choultry" (a place to offer shelter and lodging) for the poor patients visiting the Indo-American Hospital. The daily rent there was INR10- ($1 U.S. per diem). That's all!

After our children grew up and were on their own, Subhadra (my wife) and I shifted to a smaller home as that house was too big for two.

Equal Partner

It was my wife's wholehearted support that was the foundation for my ability to accomplish many things, including research, medical innovations, and teaching. Both as a woman and a doctor, she continued to be my inspiration.

With a baby in her arms, she came to the U.S, completed her residency, and climbed the ladder of success – rung by rung – so much so that she became

the Regional Director of the Physical Medicine and Rehabilitation Department, part of the Queen's Health Network. It is not an easy task to supervise almost 40 therapists, 10 attending physicians, and 30 residents!

I am not praising her because she is my wife. Rather, I can attest that she as a doctor has all sincerity and devotion towards her profession. She took an active part in raising donations for the construction and maintenance of Basava Tarakam Indo-American Cancer Hospital. Even today, she continues to work for organizations such as the South Asian and American Women Alliance (SAAWA), etc. She earned several awards for her work.

Spiritually, she has always followed her values throughout her life. She evinces great interest in understanding the meaning of holy religious hymns. She appreciates the discourses of Brahmasri Samavedam Shanmukha Sharma, a spiritual orator from the state of Andhra Pradesh. She is also a great devotee of "Vishwa yogi" Vishwamji.

With a broad-minded perspective of both the physical and the meta-physical, she believes in the adage, "Serving humanity is serving divinity." She puts that conviction into action also. Having said that, she is not an orthodox woman; she is a modern thinker. Many in the U.S. concentrate on physical fitness. Subhadra has also adopted this practice. She goes to the gym; she practices Zumba; she swims in the summer.

To sum up, Subhadra did everything for me to grow, and she worked very hard for our children to progress.

Like any other parents we did not want our children to suffer like we did in our early days. Fortunately, they appreciated our hard work and adopted good values and did well in their education.

My son Sateesh has a penchant for law. He earned his B.A. in political science from Johns Hopkins University and obtained his law degree from the renowned New York University School of Law. Although he had ample opportunities to join any corporate law firm, and make a name and a mint money, he joined as an attorney "The Legal Aid Society," primarily lending its legal services to poor people. We love the sincerity with which he has been working there for the last 20 years.

In 2015 "New York Law Journal" published an issue featuring 50 "selected" youth talents. It is needless to mention that my parental pride for my son doubled to know that the journal has named my son for this honor. The selection committee consisted of 24 judges!

My daughter-in-law, Joy, is also an academician and currently a professor of law in one of the prestigious colleges of New York.

Joy's father Mr. Raj Kanwar was a highly accomplished architect and worked in Nigeria for many years before coming to the U.S. Her parents, Ms. Vijay Kanwar and Mr. Raj Kanwar, settled in Orlando and were very respected for their community service activities.

My son and his wife have twins, a boy, Shaan Kumar Nori, and a daughter, Jhansi Nori.

My daughter, Priya, in her childhood started learning Indian classical dance, "Bharatanatyam." For 14 to 15 years, ferrying her to and from the dance classes every Sunday, which we did, was like a huge religious ritual. Priya's "Arangetram" (debut dance performance) was a colossal affair. Thereafter, she also gave a few dance performances.

When she grew up, she pursued medicine. She is now an associate professor in the department of medicine and orthopedic surgery at Albert Einstein College of Medicine. She has done all her training there. Currently, she is doing research on diseases that are caused by infections. She is one of the leading doctors in the U.S. in the treatment of Covid-19. She is also the director of one of the largest fellowship programs in the U.S. In the year 2015, she received "The Teacher of the Year" award, and in 2017, "The Rising Star" award.

Himanshu Nagar, my son-in-law, is also a renowned oncologist. He came up a hard way, like me, in his personal life. That's why I have a very special affection for him.

Himanshu's father, Ramakant Nagar, is a very fine gentleman and an individual of simple contentment. In one phrase, he is a God among humans. When he migrated to the U.S. with his family, he was a journalist and also a professional event photographer. His wife, Ms. Indrabala Nagar, was also an accomplished professional supporting him. Himanshu also used to help him by acting as a DJ (Disc Jockey) while simultaneously pursuing his studies. He was very bright in his

studies. He earned his degree in medicine at the University of Texas and obtained his post-graduate training from Cornell University Medical Center.

Priya and Himanshu have two daughters, Prana Maheswari Nagar and Abhinaya Nagar.

The children born in the U.S. are being exposed to many aspects and vagaries of life and could be easy prey to false allurement and thus tread wrong paths. Accomplished parents might not necessarily raise better children. There are many an incident where children of many reputed doctors and Nobel laureates strayed and lived disturbed lives. To share the truth, we always had a lurking fear about our children until they shone in their education and careers and were settled with their life partners. We, therefore, took great care with their upbringing. We used to take them to the temples and other cultural programs. We exposed them to Indian arts, culture, and stories with morals.

They too have nurtured good moral values, faith and devotion to God, and pursued a right path in life. They also speak good Telugu, which pleases us immensely!

One of my brothers-in-law, Subhadra's brother, is Ramesh whom we could help to come to the U.S and establish himself as a certified accountant; another, Suresh, settled with his family in Hyderabad. The "World Trade Center" was a landmark in New York known to almost everyone. The twin towers were among the tallest buildings in the world. Terrorists blasted them by planes on Sept. 11, 2001. In the morning at about 8 'o'clock, they were attacked; in two hours they were reduced into shambles. The rubble and the dust totally engulfed the nearby buildings completely and rendered them useless abodes.

My son Sateesh Nori used to live in an apartment nearby the twin towers. On the day of those attacks, my wife and I were attending to our regular duties as usual. When we had come to learn of the terrorist attack, we were dumbstruck. When we tried to contact Sateesh, that line was not functioning. We became so tense; it is difficult to describe. Early in the afternoon, Sateesh came to me. The relief and the happiness that I experienced then were also beyond words. From his apartment, he had walked almost 10 miles to reach me!

Chapter 16

MOTHER AND MOTHERLAND ARE MORE GLORIOUS THAN HEAVEN

My fourth elder brother, Nori Madhura Babu, was working in a higher post in the State Bank of India (the biggest bank owned by the govt. of India). When the employees of the bank came together and made a housing colony for themselves in the Malakpet area of Hyderabad, my brother also constructed his own house there. A separate bedroom was earmarked for my mother in his home.

with my beloved mother Sri Nori Kanaka Durgamba, in her house at Malak pet Hyderabad

My mother spent the rest of her life there. With deep devotion towards God almighty and reciting "Lalita Sahasra Namavali" (A religious book listing the thousand names of Goddess Lalita) was her undeviating daily routine. A park and a temple were also located nearby. Sitting on the veranda, looking at the passers-by, my mother used to spend her evenings.

My beloved mother Nori Kanaka Durgamba,

I must emphasize that my mother was a woman of unconditional love and compassion. She didn't admonish anyone. It is very rare that one can get along with everyone: daughters-in-law, sons-in-law, children, grandchildren. She neither used to blame any, nor was she blamed by any. She was the epitome of love. Undoubtedly, she was the center of my family.

While I was pursuing my M.D., her wrist needed minor surgery. Those who work continuously develop stiffness at the wrist and experience a pulse of shock occasionally. My mother also suffered from a painful wrist. Hence, I got her operated on and cured.

Because of that my mother used to tell everybody, "My Dattu is a big doctor," and took pride in that.

During my internship, she was found deficient in B complex. I, therefore, used to give her an injection once yearly. Although I had told her several times that it was a very small task and anybody could administer that injection for her, she never used to take it from anybody else but wait like a child for me to come and administer it.

My mother liked my kith and kin to frequent my home often, and she never used to send anybody back empty handed. She preferred to give them some gift, or something in cash or kind. I knew this and that's why whenever I visited her, I used to give her INR.50000- without fail so that she could spend it the way she liked. In turn, she used to write to

with my mother during my visit to Hyderabad from Russia.

me about who visited her when and also described their well-being, etc. Also, she used to write how much money she had had donated to which temple or what worship while meticulously enclosing the receipts. I have carefully preserved her letters and those receipts to this day.

I used to visit India four times in a year. When I informed her by phone about my upcoming visit to her, she used to feel immensely happy and wait for me expectantly. She was very fond of me and pampered me as I was the last of her children and had lost my father at a very young age. Whenever I was with her, I used to take shelter in her arms.

Once when I was in Russia, I suddenly decided to surprise her and go to India. When I called her from Hyderabad airport, she asked me, "When did you come?"!

I could not understand how she was able to guess where I was, as I had not disclosed my location to her. When I asked her the same, she brushed it aside with a smile saying, "I am your mother. Could I not know that much?" When I was in the U.S., I felt a sort of emptiness if I didn't talk to her at least once in two days.

In 1998, when I visited her in India, she was 93.

While handing over some money to her, I purposely kept away INR.4000- in my pocket and asked her to count the money I had just given to her. She counted and told me promptly,

"Dattu! It is short by 4000-; it doesn't total to INR.50000-".

At that age, her faculties were fine and mentally she was very sharp. I sheepishly smiled and confessed, "I have kept it away purposely only to test whether you would realize it or not," and handed over the rest of the money.

But then I could not realize that it was the last time that both of us would heartily laugh together. When I was about to set out, she came out and bade me "Goodbye," waving her hand.

Later, on a fateful morning, my nephew, son of my third elder brother, called me on the phone and said, "Uncle, Granny passed away."

That everyone born shall die is a universal truth known to everybody. As a doctor I witness somebody dying almost every day in the hospital. But loss of one's mother is very difficult to accept, and it causes immense sorrow. Whenever it comes to my mind, I get shaken. Until now, I cannot accept that truth. Even today, when I try to accept it, I break down inconsolably.

As soon as we got the news, Subhadra and I rushed to India. My brothers preserved her body until we reached there.

After lunch, she had developed chest pain, fatigue and ……. that was all.

After the final rites, all of us went to Nagarjuna Sagar (a multi- purpose dam across the river Krishna then in the combined state of Andhra Pradesh) and immersed her mortal remains in the river Krishna. My mother who was born on the banks of the river Krishna merged with it. On my return journey the teeming memories of my mother swarmed my mind.

When I was one year old, my mother set out to Thotavallooru from Vuyyuru with me in her arms. My sister was also there. The journey was by bullock cart. On the way, there was a bridge on Krishna canal. When the cart was going over the bridge, somehow the bullocks went haywire, and the cart driver could not control them. The bulls ran amok, and the cart suddenly turned over with a thud. Everybody in the cart sustained serious injuries. Although she was injured and started bleeding, my
mother had carefully engulfed me in her arms and saved me unscathed.

Holding me in her arms, walking my sister alongside her, she struggled to tread more than a mile to reach home! The injuries she sustained then left marks on her body for a very long time. So deep and severe were the injuries.

For our sake, she used to grind the broken rice, sold her gold bangles, and made too many more sacrifices to list -- All those incidents flashed in front of my eyes. Like the surging sea, the tears welled up in my eyes. After losing such a mother, although I still have my kith and kin, the world went blank for me.

Sometime ago, I had bought her a small table for her to dine at. That table and her spectacles and photos I carried with me back to America. In my prayer room, I keep her photo on that table. Every day during my time of worship, I pay my obeisance to her without fail.

After my mother's death, I had the misfortune of losing two of my elder brothers, my second brother Mruthyunjaya Rao 2009 and Madhura Babu 1914. They were very affectionate and loved by all. Their support to the family was remarkable. My mother lived in the house of my brother Madhurababu for most of her life happily till her last days. I am making mention about him to record his selfless services provided to our mother.

My Family

Chapter 17

HEADS OR TAILS

Success and failure are the two sides of the same coin. One cannot help feeling elated when successful or low when failing. But doctors see both birth and death from very close quarters. If they tend to feel happy about one successfully cured patient, another may not be successful. Over a period, if not totally immune to such things, they do develop a kind of sustained balance of mind.

I told you the success story about the curing of Mr. Neelam Sanjiva Reddy, the then President of India. If that was the success story, the story of my own father-in-law, Mr. Tadepalli Srinivasa Rao, father of my wife Subhadra, was a story otherwise. He developed some trouble in his lungs. He was treated initially for an infection, then for tuberculosis for some time in India. But when the investigations confirmed that it was cancer, I took him to All India Institute of Medical Sciences (AIIMS), Delhi.

Dr. Nagarur Gopinath from AIIMS was close to me. In fact, the Indian government had also sent him to New York along with President Neelam Sanjiva Reddy. He stayed with me for almost a month. He was very friendly with me. He used to be very punctual and disciplined. He was an inspiration for me. However hard he toiled throughout the day and however late he retired to bed, he used to rise early and work on his books, documentation, and research work.

It was Dr. Gopinath who had started the division of cardio-thoracic surgery at AIIMS (All India Institute of Medical Sciences), Delhi in 1964. From then, open heart surgery had become accessible for people across India. It is not a hyperbole to state that with his teaching skills he honed talent in many a student and equipped a generation of doctors in the country. Most of his students are in important positions in many reputed hospitals. Even after his retirement in 1982, he continued his relationship with AIIMS as Professor Emeritus. He did much research on cardiac ailments and encouraged his students also to do so. He was honored with "Life Achievement" awards by the Indian Association of Cardiologists and Thoracic Surgeons, etc. Recognizing his service to his country, the Indian government conferred "Padma Sri" on him in 2004

Although Professor Gopinath was a cardiac surgeon, he performed the surgery for lung cancer for my father-in-law at Delhi solely because of his affection for and friendship with me. My father-in-law recovered and left for his town. But, after three and half years, the cancer resurfaced. This time after their initial dilemma as to where to go for treatment between Delhi and the U.S, my in-laws decided to come to the U.S.

Since I had been working at Memorial Sloan-Kettering Hospital, my father-in-law wanted to get himself treated there. It is not a hospital affordable for ordinary/middle class people without insurance. It catered more to the premiers of the countries or top celebrities from various fields. My family was not able to afford the cost of treatment there. At that time, I had joined MSK very recently. My children were young yet. My savings in the bank might aggregate to hardly $1,000 U.S. while the expenses incurred for the treatment of my father-in-law were about $2,000 U.S. per day. When the doctors had lost the hope of his recovery and advised us to take him home, we did so. We paid the night nurse $200 U.S. per night.

I am at loss for words to describe how greatly tormented I was those days. I could not tell my in-laws that the expenses were much beyond my wallet; nor could I tell them to return to India. But I could not keep myself away from the problem. I was anguished as I was slowly getting sunk into deep debt. Not able to grapple with the situation, I used to take shelter among the distant, silent mountain range on the outskirts of the city. I used to breakdown into tears in that solitude.

I was caught between the human values I cherish on one side and my poor financial status on the other. The trains of thought as a doctor on one, and as a son-in-law on the other, tormented me. I could not share this even with my wife. I was filled with anxiety. After a few days, his condition worsened, and we admitted him to the hospital again. After two weeks in ICU (Intensive Care Unit), he died in 1981. With a heavy heart, my mother-in-law returned to India. My home was filled with gloom and a kind of eerie silence.

When I resumed my duties, Mr. John Glenn, the chief of the finance department of the hospital, called for me. The bill for my father-in-law's treatment had come to over $60,000 U.S.

"What are you going to do?" he inquired.

"By no means, can I afford it," was my answer.

I decided to meet Dr. Samuel Hellman, our physician-in-chief, who was also very fond of me, my research, and my patient care, to request that he help me. Upon my request, he called the accounts officer and instructed him to waive as much of the charges as possible. With that, my debt had been considerably reduced and the rest of the bill I paid in installments. This is an example as to how the tides and ebbs quickly follow one another in life.

Chapter 18

FAMILIAL BOND

Recently, on the 90th birthday of my eldest brother, Nori Radhakrishna Murthy, we had a cozy and eventful celebration and family get- together at Hyderabad.

That day, I posed him a question, "Dear Brother! Within a few days after your getting a job, our father died. Did it overwhelm you with the impending responsibilities?"

"No, I can't say so, but, certainly, it was a huge commitment on my tender shoulders. I would need to be able to support my brothers and sisters. I needed to get them proper education and get all of them married and settled in life. The only haunting thought that continually goaded me was how I should endeavor to address the situation. As a

my brothers and sisters in law.
Bottom row L-R Smt. Madhavi, Smt. Kanaka Durga, Smt. Sri Lakshmi,
Smt. Satya Vani, Smt. Suguna Devi, Smt. Subhadra Nori.

lecturer in the National College at Machilipatnam (Bundar- a port town in Andhra Pradesh), my salary was INR120-(about $1.50 U.S.) per month – hardly sufficient to make both ends meet. Mr. Varadacharyulu was the chairman of the college. He was staying at Gudur. I went to him and pleaded for a hike in my salary as I had the education of five brothers and marriages of two sisters at stake. He took pity upon me and increased my salary to INR 150- (almost $2 U.S.) per month. That

at a celebratory function for my eldest brother with the rest of my family bottom row: sister Rama Devi, Satya Vani sister-in-law, Mr. Radha Krishna Mur- thy, the eldest brother, Lanka Satyanarayana Sastry brother-in-law. Standing row L-R Lanka Madhusudhan Sharma brother-in-law, Madhura Babu brother, Madhavi sister-in-law, myself Rama Theerdha brother, Indra Devi sister, Ramamohan
Rao, brother Sri Lakshmi sister-in-law and Suguna Devi sister-in-law.

with my brother, Shri Nori Rama Theerdha at the space Museum Washington DC.

was a big amount those days," answered my brother with a heavy sigh, wiping the tears from his welled-up eyes.

While listening to this, we also felt very heavy at heart. All of us were in tears. Almost all of us were in our 70s, but, recalling those difficult days, we could not control our emotions. Those struggles bonded us so strongly. That affectionate relationship among us had nurtured our values in life.

To make the mood lighter, somebody cracked a joke, recalling this story.

During my second brother's wedding, an Ambassador (a car brand from India) was ready to set out from Thotavallooru to Vijayawada. A child, I insisted on traveling in that car as they tried to dissuade me, "You are a small kid. Why do you want to accompany the bridegroom? Come by the next bus." Then they pushed me out. But, I, being very stubborn, travelled by the same car anyway, holding on to the door and almost standing on only one leg all through the distance.

"Dattu was an impossible guy then and of course now also." Everybody broke into peals of laughter.

top: at the Begumpet airport Hyderabad sent off to America in 1976. L-R Mr Kota Nagendra Prasad, myself, my wife, a friend, is holding my son, my elder sister-in-law, Smt. Nori Satya Vani, my eldest brother Shri Nori Radha Krishna Murthy, Nori Sreenivas, and Nori Chandrashekhar.

That heart-filled laughter helped us to get relief.

I must mention more about my eldest brother Sri Radhaskrishna Murthy and my sister in law smt. satyavani. They fulfilled all duties expected of them providing required support and guidance to all our family members. They performed marriages of my last two sisters and four brothers including me in a dignified manner. Particular mention needs to be made about my two brother in laws, Lanka Satyanarayana Sastry and Lanka madhusudhana sarma. Both are exceptionally good and very pious and family oriented. I am happy to mention that all their children and my brother's children also settled well.

My brothers too progressed well in their respective professions. My eldest brother retired from service as Inspector general of police. Brother Mrutyunjaya Rao M. A. retired as senior officer in labor department. Brother Mohan Rao MSc PhD, retired as deputy director in institute of preventive medicine (IPM). Brother Madhura babu, M.A. retired as General manager of State Bank of India. Brother Ramatheerdha, M.A. retired as Chief General manager in Andhra Pradesh state cooperative Bank.

Chapter 19

PARAGON OF BEAUTY

"Mirror, mirror on the wall, who is the prettiest of all?" If someone asks, the mirror in India would say "Sridevi." Sridevi, a film artist from India, epitomized beauty as well as acting skills.

This is the story of her mother, Rajeswari.

Born in Tirupathi, a temple town (which houses the second richest religious site in the world), Rajeswari aspired to become a film artist. What she could not become herself, she could vicariously attain through her daughter Sridevi. Debuting in the film world as a child artist, Sridevi quickly evolved as a famous film heroine in the Southern film world (it

consists of Tollywood of Telugu, Kollywood of Tamil,

at my Padma Shri award celebration organized by Dr Shri T Subbi Rami Reddy. featured Mr Reddy, Mr Boney Kapoor, the legendary Bollywood actress Sridevi Kapoor, Sateesh nori, my wife and I

Mollywood of Malayalam and Sandalwood of Kannada). It hardly took any time for her to enter Bollywood of Hindi and conquer Northern India also. All through this journey, Rajeswari always accompanied Sridevi and took great care of her.

If I recollect, it was perhaps in 1995, when Sridevi had been very busy in shootings, during the filming of "Judai," Rajeswari fainted on the sets. The prognosis pointed to brain cancer. The doctors at

Madras (now

legendary Bollywood actress Sridevi Kapoor speaking at the Reception function in New Delhi.

Chennai) advised that she go to Memorial Sloan Kettering Hospital at New York for the best treatment as she required surgery. Hence, they had come to New York.

Normally, whenever a patient comes from India to the U.S, they would, firstly, consult me. Similarly, Sridevi and her mother also tried to do the same. But I was overseas attending a conference at that time.

Hence, the hospital organized an appointment for her with another doctor.

A neurosurgeon examined all of her scans and decided for surgery.

On May 26, before her being taken into the operating theater, she had reportedly been very scared and had tightly held Sridevi's hand and asked her to request "the doctors to properly perform the surgery." The family doctor who had accompanied them allegedly had smiled with a repartee, "They would only do it properly. To tell the doctors to perform the surgery properly is like advising your daughter to act well."

But fate had failed her. Rajeswari's worst fears had come true!

Sridevi Kapoor affectionately honoring me with a shawl at the function

Although the neurosurgeon was an experienced professional, he did not correctly verify who she was before the surgery as the patients had been swapped. The result: although she had a tumor on one side of the brain, he incised on the other side and prepared for surgery. But he could not find any tumor there. After further examination, he realized his mistake.

The hospital management revealed the mistake to Sridevi. Most of the important newspapers, including the "New York Times," carried the news in prominent headlines. The hospital suspended the doctor. A case was filed in court. The American president Bill Clinton also responded and further tightened restrictions on the hospitals.

In the meanwhile, I returned from my conference and resumed my duties. I found a note on my desk about Sridevi's telephone call to me. I returned her call. I learned the details of the case. They also came and consulted me. As they had lost confidence in Memorial Sloan Kettering, they shifted Rajeswari to Cornell Hospital where I was working.

During that time, Sridevi became close to me.

Although Sridevi used to dominate with her screen presence, in real life she was very shy and was very hesitant to talk to any outsider.

legendary actress Sharmila Tagore honoring me at my Padma Shri award celebration.

Her mother was her world. Therefore, her mother's sickness and such a brazen mistake in the treatment thereof by an internationally reputed hospital shell shocked her.

"Without my mother, I am nothing, Doctor! Will she recover?" She used to ask me very naively. "I should have gotten her treated by the best doctors in Madras. Perhaps I have made a mistake. I am totally lost here and feeling very lonely," she used to lament with a kind of remorse. She also affirmed, "I am glad that God has shown you to me to help me."

During those difficult days, Boney Kapoor stood by her like a rock. While overseeing the treatment of Rajeswari, he attended the court hearings regarding the surgery and also for the compensation for the error. Four years ago, in 1991, when Sridevi's father had died, Boney Kapoor had also greatly helped her to come out of her bereavement.

Whatever had happened, she was no way responsible for the hospital's mistake and her mother would surely recover – both were the facts. But to tell that to her and console her took a lot of time and effort. Only when explained in detail, what the future course of treatment would be and what the results would be and how those would help her mother to recover, did she get some solace.

Assuaged of her fears, she saw her mother's surgery done "correctly" and also meticulously got her the required radiation therapy. Rajeswari would recover within 6 to 8 weeks.

"A highly reputed hospital of North America has made a blunder. It is injustice to the patient. As another reputed hospital of the country, let us correct that mistake and render justice. Also, it is not proper to charge them for this." This was my stand with the hospital and we, at Cornell Hospital, did not charge.

Within that brief span of time, Sridevi had become very close to me as if she were my own little sister.

In spite of such nerve-wracking tension, she still flew to India to participate in the shoot of a Malayalam movie "Deva Ragam" because its director Bharatan was the one who had given Sridevi her first break as an artist in an ad (for a soap brand, Chandrikaa). Such was her integrity and character!

After her mother was discharged, she continued to be treated as an out-patient. During those days, Sridevi used to visit my home. Although she was very reticent, she used to open up with me freely. If once she developed some trust in somebody, she would be comfortable. She developed that trust in and affinity with me. Though she was a superstar for the outside world, she was very much childlike at my home.

In my office, despite my request, she would be very hesitant to sit in my chair. Suddenly, she would break into a tete-a-tete. While we both continued to converse in Telugu, Boney Kapoor used to discuss business with his distributors. Sometimes when she started to reprimand him, he would say laughingly, "Doctor Saab! The antenna has opened up. Let me run away now."

Rajeswari recovered and they left for India. But they have not forgotten me. She often used to phone me. Whether to marry Boney or not? What would be the consequences?... She had many such lurking doubts and used to discuss them with me for 2 or 3 hours, sometimes on a daily basis. I could not tell her anything for certain but assisted in her thought process.

With Sri Devi At My House in Scarsdale, New York

Whenever I visited them in India, they treated me with special care. They organized very good vegetarian meals for me. Her mother also gave me some rare photographs of Sridevi, which are not available to anyone else, such as her "Arangetram" (debut of classical dance) photographs.

The year following her treatment, in 1996, Sridevi and Boney Kapoor solemnized their marriage in a simple ceremony with a very few guests. When I went to India, I met them. They took me to "Taj Coramandal" at Chennai for lunch. It was just the three of us. Sridevi used to eat very little. I would often chide her, "How can you survive eating so little?"" But she used to relish eating "gongura" (Red sorrel leaves. Gongura is a leafy plant, which has many culinary uses, mostly popular in the Telugu states). That day she complained that she had pain in the stomach as if she were carrying a stone. Nevertheless, she could eat almost triple her normal intake.

"No, it is not any stone. Perhaps, it's a baby. The way you ate today suggests that you are probably carrying a child. "Better get yourself tested," I said to her. It was prophetic. She was confirmed pregnant.

When Jhanvi and Khushi were born, she felt elated. She sent their pictures to me. After 3 or 4 years, her mother Rajeswari died of other ailments. After her mother, Sridevi had given me the next place in her hierarchy of relationships. I can attest to that with certainty.

Thereafter, also, whenever Sridevi used to come to the U.S for any film shooting, we used to meet and spend time together talking. She visited our temple of Shirdi Saibaba I have had built in the U.S. Whenever I was in Mumbai and wanted to visit Shirdi, a nearby temple town, she used to lend me her car, pack my breakfast by 4 am, and inquire about my well-being, once calling the driver every 2 or 3 hours.

My friends who knew my closeness to her often used to ask me, "Can we come to your home? Can we give her some type of tribute??" That closeness only prompted us to invite her as a guest to a TANA (Telugu Association of North America) conference that took place in Los Angeles. Before she was invited to the dais, my daughter, Priya, made a brief introduction of her to an audience of almost 10,000. Also an audio-visual made by me of about four minutes of her performances gleaned from several of her movies was shown. Sridevi told me later that she was delighted by both. ANR (Akkineni Nageswara Rao, the perennial hero of the Telugu film world) had also come as a guest to the same conference. In his eloquent speech he shared many good things about Sridevi.

We invited her as a guest once more for the celebrations of American Independence Day. "Doctor! Kindly tell me what should be appropriate for my speech for this occasion?" she requested and took notes. The way she delivered the speech in front of the audience and her later speech during the VIP supper were excellent! I was able to witness first hand how she reportedly undergoes a metamorphosis in front the camera. She was cool but very intelligent.

Whenever I praised her saying, "Oh! You are very talented!" She used to laugh it away and say to me, "No doctor! It is all the magic of the camera."

Once when we were at Hyderabad, we learned that Sridevi

was also there in town for a shoot. My wife Subhadra and her friends, thoroughly decked out, went to meet her.

After returning, my wife burst into continuous laughter as she narrated the scene: "All of us had donned so much make-up while she was totally devoid of make-up. When we took some snaps along with her, she looked like a queen, all of us like her entourage." So enchanting was the beauty of Sridevi.

She never used to fail to be in touch with me wherever I was and made it a point to meet me if I were at Dubai.

Once she told her daughter young Jhanvi, "Hey Jhanvi! You should also become a famous doctor like Sir." Jhanvi was equally naughty and paid a repartee, "Yes, certainly, if not in real life, in a movie I would portray that role."

After a long gap, Sridevi came for a shoot in Manhattan, New York, as she was the star of a Hindi film, "English Vinglish." She used to return from the shoot very tired about 9 or 10 pm, and we used to send her some freshly cooked hot South Indian fare such as "Puli Hora" (a rice item made with the paste of tamarind, sesame seeds, peppers and other spices), "Idli," "Sambar," etc. Her hard work did not go to waste. The movie was a huge success. She was also very happy with the result.

Normally, over the course of time, friends and siblings also, on a day-to-day basis, get out of touch as they are busy with the mundane affairs of their own family. I was no exception in regard to Sridevi. I became a little complacent thinking that she had been happy with her family and children.

In the meanwhile, the ghastly news of her death became viral. India has lost its favorite actress and heroine. The impact on me is different: I have lost my little sister.

I went to console Boney Kapoor, her husband. Her home was like a temple without its deity!

That family continues to be in touch with me. He sends me the published articles and write-ups about her. The children show me a great deal of respect. My blessings are there for them as are my efforts to console them, but my loss is irreplaceable.

Chapter 20
DEAR LOVELY FRIENDS (DLF)

It is commonly believed that Mr. Chaudhary Raghavendra Singh was the pioneer of the real estate business in India. It was he who founded DLF (Delhi Land and Finance) in 1946. His daughter Indira Singh was married to Mr. K.P. Singh (Kushal Pal Singh) of the Indian Army. Mr.
K.P. Singh who had worked earlier as an aeronautical engineer in the United Kingdom, backed by sufficient experience, left the army and joined DLF. The visionary couple would grow the company into a multi-crore (multi-million dollar) corporation and remain at the top of the construction industry.

The concept of creating residential colonies from the land of the farmers and sharing the profits with the original owners was initiated and implemented solely by the Singhs. Creating the necessary facilities for the construction laborers and mainly focusing on their health and well-being, Indira Singh adopted their villages and spend a great deal of money to render needful services to them.

Unfortunately, Indira Singh suffered from lung cancer. Initially, the couple went to London. There they were told that it was nearly impossible to completely cure her. Hence, they searched for the best hospital for her treatment and eventually landed at MSK Cancer Center. Since my name was recommended by the team of doctors treating her, she was brought to me. While treating her, I got acquainted with the Singhs.

They were the wealthiest "Jat" (a caste from Punjab) family in the whole of the world. But their wealth did not affect them. Both K.P. Singh and Indira Singh were so humble that nobody could hazard a guess at their riches.

When I mentioned it to them, this was their simple refrain: "We were not born rich, Doctor! We created wealth working relentlessly day and night and steadfastly endured all impediments." In his autobiography, "Whatever the Odds, the Incredible Story Behind DLF,' Mr. Singh wrote about me.

Mrs. Singh recovered and returned to India. After almost 18 years, she was diagnosed with another type of cancer. This time, because of

with Mrs. Indira Singh, wife of Shri KP Singh chairman of DLF at their 65th wedding anniversary in New Delhi. Also seen from left-to-right are Mrs. Darshan Bains, legendary actress Sharmila Tagore and others.

her age, she was unable to travel to the U.S. Also, an earlier helicopter crash, in which she had been involved and had consequently suffered multiple fractures, compounded her current clinical status. Hence she was restricted to her home. Mr. Singh called me to brief me about her. He inquired whether I could travel to India to treat her second primary cancer.

He promised to make necessary arrangements. I was expecting airline tickets.

He sent me a private jet!!

I was dumbfounded. I set out from New York to India. My colleague Dr. Manjit Singh Bains accompanied me. When the flight stopped at London for refueling, I was lost in my thoughts. It was a strange feeling to fly by a private jet to treat a patient in my motherland where I had started my life journey in an impoverished family.

With Sri K.P. Singh D L F

I visited and examined Mrs. Singh but could not save her because of her advanced age and cancer. In February 2018, Indira Singh bade adieu to this world.

Mr. Singh and the entire family have been grateful that I was able to give her a lengthy extension of life after her first bout with cancer. Wherever I am, the now nonagenarian Mr. Singh keeps in touch with me and visits me whenever he is in the U.S.

*

Mr. Singh's letter

I have read in newspapers that the State Government of Andhra Pradesh had recommended the name of Dr Nori Dattatreyudu for one of the highest civilian honors "Padma" awards. I am one of those front rankers who wholeheartedly support such move. He earned international repute as a specialist doctor who cured many a cancer patient. He is a very successful radiation oncologist. By relentlessly taking part in the medical research, he was instrumental in spreading his knowledge. His innovative methods of radio therapy have won the acceptance of many.

I know Dr Nori for the last 16 years. When my wife Indira suffered from the lung cancer, we have scouted for appropriate treatment. We have consulted many doctors and visited many hospitals. Everywhere, we could only hear "She can't be cured. At the most, she may live only for another two years. But some doctors both in England and the
U.S suggested consulting Dr Nori as a last resort. We did not want to lose that option. Then, I came to know about Dr Nori. We met him in the Presbyterian hospital of New York. After his treatment, my wife Indira recovered. She lived long thereafter – healthy and happy. Science may not be magic. But Dr Nori is a very good doctor and in his dexterous hands modern medicine can work miracles, I started believing since then.

I may not hesitate to state that Dr Nori is a wonderful doctor. He uses available modern knowledge to treat the patients. He uses different, appropriate treatment for every single patient. Either in winning the trust of the patients or instill self-confidence in them, he stands in the forefront. By the time the treatment is completed, and the patient is
recovered, he becomes a member the patient's family; a lifelong friend who walks along indeed.

In my opinion he is not only a great doctor but a great humanitarian and a spiritual thinker. When I was invited for the inauguration of the Sai temple in Baldwin's of New York, I could get acquainted with the unparalleled devotee in him. To build a temple like the one in Shirdi, the help of his wife Dr Subhadra was also immense. The way he interacts with his colleague doctors or others in his team, he reminds us a capable C.E.O.

Despite such credentials, he doesn't forget his roots – not even in his sleep. The professional expertise, spiritual thinking, generosity, he longs to deploy for the use of his mother land – India. He wishes the Indian youth to shine in all walks of life. Based on the preaching of Saibaba, the Indian Saint, philosopher and Guru, he strives to accomplish spiritual progress.

If our country is shining on the world arena, it is because of the India's own capable children like Dr Nori Dattatreyudu.

Blessings and Divine Blessings to

CHIRANJEEVI DR. NORI DATTATREYUDU

With divine love and your unstinted resolve, you have reached pinnacles of success, and your ambition to spread the message of universal love and love for all the mentors of the world is nothing but the wish of the Viswaguru Dattatreya.

The title for your autobiography is apt since you have risen above time, with obedience, patience, overcoming the difficult times and won both the time and also the hearts of the public with whom you have come into contact in your life.

Defeating the difficulties coming across at various stages of your life, you reached this stage by molding yourself. That is the secret of your success. The Sanskrit saying that (of hard work never gets wasted) is well suited to your life. Your ambition and noble thoughts to produce documentary film on the role of mother in shaping the future of individuals is highly laudable and my blessings for the success in your endeavor. You have become a role model and influenced millions to follow your path. Your struggles in your profession and the way you have overcome with confidence and with the blessings of your parents, teachers and Viswaguru Dattatreya is inspirational.

Your love for your mother, your wife, family and your commitment to give solace to the troubled, cancer patients and your servitude need to be recognized by all the Governments, UNO and people of the world. Your autobiography is no doubt a torch bearer and you have shown a path, in which the youth of the world have to follow and make the world a better place to live in. I wish you all the best and success in your endeavor. I wish that your autobiography be translated into English and other languages to inspire many more people.

Chapter 21

MY SPIRITUAL GURUS

with our Sadguru Sri Sri Sri Sri, Vishwa Yogi VishwamJi Maharaj. Swamiji was honoring my wife and me at a function which was organized by Swamiji in Hyderabad.

Everybody has a chance to render service to others in their own individual way. Their utilizing that chance is the real worship. That is the path of salvation. "Service to mortals is service to Madhav (The Lord)." Many "Gurus" guided me in this path. The most important one of them was Sri Vishwa yogi Vishwamji Maharaj.

He was my guiding light and showed many miracles to me. I fervently believe that his blessings certainly helped me to come this far. He was born on Mar 5, 1944 n the city of Guntur in the state of Andhra Pradesh, India. His father was Anjaneyulu and mother Varalakshmamma. Like my father, Nori Satyanarayana, Anjaneyulu was also very spiritual and used to meditate. Lord Dattatreya appeared in his dream and initiated

him with "Taraka Mantra." He was a poet

Sri Sri Sri Vishwa Yogi Vishwamji Maharaj at our new house in Long Island New York.

and led his life upholding high values. On a certain occasion, he was to stay in the holy city of Kashi (Benares). One night, the rays of light emitting from the "Jyotir lingam" (scintillating phallus, a manifestation of Lord Vishwanatha, the reigning deity of Kashi) flashed before him. At the same time, his wife at Guntur delivered a baby boy. Anjaneyulu, therefore, named that boy as Vishwanatha Sastry. During his childhood, the boy was called Vishwam by everybody.

Vishwanatha Sastry completed his B.A. in Mathematics and B.Ed. and worked as a teacher for some time. He earned recognition as a good teacher of mathematics and English, earned commendations from his higher officers, and served as a model to other teachers too.

In 1965, Sri Dattatreya Wadekar Maharaj, the disciple of popular spiritual guru Sridhar Maharaj conferred a spiritual initiation on him. He also transferred the entirety of his spiritual powers to Vishwamji. To put them to proper use, Vishwamji undertook intensive penance for 21 years and augmented his spiritual prowess achieving the metamorphosis of himself into a living saint. People started addressing him so, as Vishwamji Maharaj. In November 188, he resigned from his teacher's position and established a hermitage near Kondaveedu and started his full-fledged spiritual life advocating for the welfare of the world. Devotees believe that he is the 9th incarnation of Lord Dattatreya. In my practice of spirituality, two Gurus continue to guide me in every step. One is the Shirdi Sainath in Samadhi; another is Vishwamji Maharaj, a living incarnation of a saint. Apart from sincerely paying my obeisance to them, what else I can give them in return? Anyone can know where to start and how far to grow in life.

If to determine the target and to attain it in the proper way is one part; continually watching our direction and effecting a course correction whenever necessary is another one.

That is an art. We shall learn it.

After my 70th birthday, I decided to make certain changes in my lifestyle. Instead of rushing through life, I have decided to work more intensively for the benefit of society and for the betterment of my motherland, India.

As a first step in that direction, I stepped down from the chairmanship of the radiation oncology department of New York Hospital Medical Center of Queens as well as from the directorship of its cancer center. The next year, i.e., in 2019, I also stepped down from the chairmanship of Weill Cornell Medical College and the Presbyterian Hospital of New York. Stepping down is neither resignation nor retirement.

By then, I had been managing all those three posts for the last 25 years. It was not that I was clamoring for a post. I worked very hard to develop the New York Hospital Medical Center of Queens for about ten years. To put it in correct perspective, the center was like my foster daughter. I was afraid to hand it over to anybody because of my lurking fear of their becoming negligent towards it and instead doggedly worked for its betterment.

When I look back, it appeared to be a correct decision. Of course, the alternative could have been to entrust it to somebody else and reduce my burden. Anyway, bygones are bygones! I continue to teach at these institutions and do research. And give guest lectures to disseminate the gist of my experience and the knowledge I acquired over the years.

In my childhood, my elder brother Madhura Babu consulted a Nadi astrologer to find out about my future. (In India, there are several kinds of prophecy tellers who examine the palm or face.)

He predicted that I would become a doctor and set out to America, etc. with exact dates too! But later, I would come to serve the patients in front of the temple of Kapaleeswara (an incarnation of the Hindu God, one of the triumvirates, Lord Shiva) in Madras (now renamed as Chennai). We could not comprehend such prophecy then.

In 2019, at the request of Dr. Pratap C. Reddy, the chairman of Apollo Hospitals, one of the largest medical conglomerates of India, I accepted the role of International Director of that organization. When I visited Apollo's primary office at Chennai, which is near Kapaleeswara temple, I immediately recollected the prophecies made by that astrologer!! Nowadays, I frequent the center at Chennai. Apollo has 14 cancer centers across the country, and I guide them to impart appropriate treatment for prevention, mitigation, and curing of cancer.

I also visit the highly reputed Tata Memorial Hospital in Mumbai and AIIMS, All India Institute of Medical Sciences, whenever required.

I have a firm belief in the Sanskrit adage, "Yaa Devee sarva bhooteshu, vritti roopena samsthitha," which means that the omnipresent power of the Almighty exists in one's profession. Whether it is in the calling of a teacher, doctor, potterer, or a barber, the level of occupation in the societal hierarchy does not matter. (In India, the hierarchy of chaturvarna, or four strata, of occupations has been prevalent from ancient times.) No matter the level, as long as one sincerely pursues one's calling, the Almighty would certainly grace him.

I often used to visit Shirdi in Maharashtra state to experience "Darshan" (a glimpse of) Saibaba.

I used to if a cancer center was opened there, it would have catered to the poor and the needy in that area. How it could be made possible at Shirdi was my continual deliberation. My logic was that if God is found in the work, my work could also be found at God's abode.

Baba made my dream come true through Mr. Radhakrishna Vikhe Patil. Mr. Radhakrishna Patil was the M.L.A. (Member of Legislative Assembly) of Shirdi constituency. He was also the Minister for Housing in the cabinet of the state of Maharashtra.

Ahmed Nagar was a part of his constituency. Had the political equations not gone awry, he would have become the Chief Minister of that state. Patil's father Ekanta Rao (Balasaheb Vikhe Patil) served as Finance Minister in the Indian central government. Also, he was conferred with Padma Bhushan for his social service. His father, grandfather of Radhakrishna Patil, Vittal Rao Vikhe Patil was also a Padmashri award recipient. He is reputed to have started the first sugar mill in Asia run by the farmers through a cooperative movement.

When one of this family's members was affected by cancer, they came to America. That's how, first his son Sujay, and then Radhakrishna Patil himself became acquainted with me. Gradually, we have become friends. I came to know that they already had a trust founded after Mr. Vittal Rao Vikhe Patil which used to run engineering, medical, nursing and dental colleges.

Among them, Pravara Institute of Medical Sciences quickly grew into an esteemed university. Patil's family invited me to the institute and made me its chief scientific advisor and chief patron. Whenever I visited the institute, they always made me sit in the seat of president and expressed their love and respect.

There is a hospital of 1,000 beds in Shirdi affiliated with Pravara. I have a particular affinity towards the oncology department there. I also organize the fellowships for the students of the college at Basava Tarakam Indo-American Cancer Center in Hyderabad. The C.E.O of our cancer center, Dr. R.V. Prabhakar Rao, is another devotee of Baba. He also wished "to do something good for the post-graduate students of Shirdi" and hence wholeheartedly worked with me on this project.

The Patil family was so immensely happy when I was conferred with Padmashri by the Union Government of India. They invited me to Shirdi and honored me there. Shirdi was inundated with billboards featuring me. Seeing them, I felt that Baba himself was honoring me.

More than that, my prayer for a cancer center for the locals and good education for the students of that area was heard by Baba, who enabled me to realize that dream by bringing the Patil family closer to me. Baba had rendered true the adage, "Service to humanity is service to the Almighty."

On one occasion, I came out of a Delhi hotel and was waiting for a car in the portico. There was a group of MPs (Members of Parliament) nearby. Perhaps they had come to attend the parliament. One of them rushed towards me and despite my efforts to stop him, touched my feet. It was Mr. Kanumoori Bapiraju.

He fondly introduced me to others as "the doctor who treated my mother." I learned that he was the chairman of Tirumala Tirupathi Devasthanam (TTD) Board (Tirupathi, with the reigning deity Lord Venkateshwara, is the second richest religious center in the world and the richest in India). He invited me to Tirumala (hilly abode of the Lord), personally organized and accompanied me to the "darshan" (glimpse) of the Lord (normally, it takes a few hours to have a glimpse of the deity) and arranged for the Lord's sacred offerings, the "prasadam." Also, the then Executive Officer of TTD, Mr. L.V. Subramanyam, took me to Alimelu Mangapuram (The nearby suburb, the abode of the Lord's consort, Alimelu) and facilitated participation in the Goddess' "Brahmotsavam."

If this is not a divine blessing, then what is??

Whatever we do and whatsoever greatness we accomplish, we are only the tools of the God Almighty.

Often the adage "Naaham Kartaa, Hari Kartaa" ("I am not doing anything, but the Lord is the doer") is vindicated.

There remain a few tasks I wanted to do but could not do until now. A few cancers can be detected early. If we can spread that awareness and rout them out without a trace, it would be good.

One large foundation shall be started to help children.

Shirdi Baba at our mandir New York

When mothers die of cancer; many children are being orphaned. I feel that these children should be given shelter, be educated, and be given help to stand on their own legs. In my profession, I have seen many cancer-affected mothers who were bothered more about the future of heir children in their absence than about their own recovery from cancer. My dream is to allay their fears and assure them that the future of their children will be safe and secure, even in their absence. My goal is to establish a not- for-profit foundation for these children.

I also wish to make a documentary on "mother's love," if any Bollywood or Tollywood artists, directors, or music directors come forward to do that. How every mother in nature strives for her children with unconditional love, how she toils beyond her limits. For example, one type of penguin, though small in size, swims miles together to catch fish for her little ones. When I learned of this and witnessed it during my trip to South Africa I could not stop my tears. I feel like showing to the whole world the place of a mother in one's life by capturing such beings' endeavors and love for their little ones. I also would like to incorporate in the documentary what the premiers of nations, scientists, and spiritual leaders have to say about their mothers.

All the above tasks, I may not be able to attain entirely on my own. Those dreams require the support of governments and important personalities coming together to achieve them. But I am confident that one day, I will surely accomplish them.

Body, mind, and heart are interlinked with one another. If one is not all right, the rest won't work well. Hence, keeping our thought process clear can help to lead a healthy lifestyle. For that, I offer valuable suggestions -- nine of them. Shall we call them "Navratnas," or Nine gems?

1. Life shall have a clear definition. We shall have clarity about what
we want to do, what we want to accomplish.

2. We shall clearly focus. To achieve our objective, we shall divide the process into smaller fragments and prioritize which objective should be executed first and which follows next, etc. We shall concentrate on the most important task first.

3. Time is money. We shall use it efficaciously; never squander it. We shall invest time intelligently. We shall keep learning what is useful to us. We shall also keep ourselves up to date with the developments in the domain we have selected. We shall not procrastinate on tasks. Time frittered away can't be reclaimed.

4. We shall work hard. Success doesn't come easily. It won't come to us if we are idle. Whatever we do, we shall do it with 100% dedication.

5. We must not be stubborn in expecting that everything happens as we wish. It is better to plan on a macro level but make necessary amendments when required.

6. By not being practical and flexible and not facing reality, we may not accomplish the objective. We may despair. And very often, we may not accomplish what we want.

7. Unexpected opportunities may knock on our door. If we are alert, we can take advantage of them. We shall be prepared to face such twists in life.

8. We shall not shy away from taking a risk. We shall plan to address the obstacles and impediments we may encounter. We shall not have any fear of failure. Failures teach us lessons, add experience.

9. The most important thing is that we shall accomplish our objectives on the foundation of our moral values. We shall respect our fellow human beings and mother nature. However rich or famous we may be, without values such status is hollow, empty. There is no happiness. Only when heart, mind, and soul work in tandem can happiness be obtained. If we can feel proud of ourselves whenever we look at ourselves in the mirror, that is the real Success. We shall be triumphant!

As I mentioned in the very first chapter, my father was a teacher, a spiritual leader, a religious orator, and a philosopher. During one of my recent visits to India, I was able to get hold of one of his personal notes. As I prepare now for the years ahead, I would like to share with you a part of my legacy from my father.

"Always observe economy of time…speech…. money…and energy. Always examine yourself to see if there lies within you a nobler thought…a sweeter word…and a kind and better action."

Chapter 22

THE PEOPLE WHO INSPIRED ME

As a part of my profession, I had the opportunity to treat not only Americans and Indians but also patients from other countries. In about 45 years of my professional voyage, I was able to meet many people and also had the opportunity to come to know about their personal and professional lives.

Everybody evinces interest about celebrities. Let me also share certain things about some of them, not only because these are interesting but also because they present a few lessons about life, as well as medical warnings.

These patient stories might be but a few passages in my autobiography. But they cover diverse talents of many a field and their triumph against cancer. From India, Nargis Dutt, the Heroine of the Hindi film world, with a film like "Mother India" to her credit, was well-known not only to the Hindi audience but also across the country and abroad with a huge fan following. She ruled the Hindi film world for more than thirty years. Almost all the films in which she acted with Raj Kapoor were big hits. When the Best Actress award was introduced at the National level, she was the first recipient. She married Sunil Dutt, who braved his life to save her from a fire accident that occurred during the filming of "Mother India." They have a son, Sanjay Dutt and two daughters Namrata and Priya. It was an idyllic life until then.

In 1979, during the proceedings of the upper house of parliament (Rajya Sabha) of which she was a member, she suddenly fell sick. She was taken from Delhi to Mumbai to admit her to Breach Candy Hospital there. Observing minor symptoms like itching around the stomach, doctors initially felt that she had had jaundice, but in the final diagnosis it was to be pancreatic cancer.

In that stage, she was brought to Memorial Sloan Kettering Cancer Center. She was cured of cancer after surgery and radiation. She returned to Mumbai. But she had become very weak. On 1981 May 1, she was again admitted to the hospital. Contrary to the prevalent belief, her cancer had not reoccurred.

She had a urinary tract/duct infection

With Mr. Scott Carpenter. One of the Mercury seven astronauts at my office in Manhattan, New York. He Came in for a consultation.

and consequently, went into a coma and died after 2 days. She was
hardly.

In her memory, her husband Sunil Dutt founded Nargis Dutt Memorial Cancer Foundation. On its behalf, he would actively participate in the management of Tata Memorial Hospital. I really liked them. They were an ideal couple. I watched Sunil Dutt treating his wife like an angel.

Nargis, in spite of her being a star, never used to put on any airs. She loved her family, especially her son, Sanjay Dutt. While she was in the hospital in New York, she recorded a message on how to behave as a good son and sent it to him. It is believed that the message worked on him and it was a turning point in his life.

According to medical science, I often say, "Listen to the Body." Nargis Dutt's case vindicated how important this advice is. When symptoms surface, even in a minor way, immediate care should be taken.

Mr Carpenter in an astronaut space-suit presented me with an **autographed photo**

I had a colleague Dr. Jatin P. Shah at MSK Cancer Center in New York. He is an expert in head and neck surgery. He completed his medicine degree at Baroda Medical College, Vadodara, Gujarat.

He learned that Dr. Kothari, who had been his professor in surgery, was diagnosed with prostate cancer. He immediately brought him to the
U.S. to be treated by me for his cancer. Prof. Kothari was 75 years old and he did not have adequate medical insurance that could take care of his treatment. Considering his age and health condition, I designed an innovative and the least
expensive out-patient Brachytherapy treatment. He received his out-patient cancer treatment in the morning and returned to India the next day. Dr Jatin Shah thanked me profusely for saving his professor's life.

Before leaving he complimented me and blessed me and praised me as "Doctor of Doctors." He died of natural causes at the age of 90.

But the type of treatment I had designed for him has become a standard of care and one of the options in the treatment of prostate cancer.

Yash Chopra is a very familiar name to Hindi film lovers. His films normally consist of the predominance of women (heroine) characters, high voltage human emotions, the lifestyle of the wealthy, good music, and mostly picturesque locales of Switzerland. Mrs. Pamela Chopra was the wife of that popular producer and director of many a hit movie. She was a singer and used to assist as a lyricist. Mrs. Pamela was initially diagnosed with breast cancer. As it was not treated well in time, it had spread to her brain. Eventually, she suffered paralysis, losing the mobility of a hand and a leg. She was initially taken to London for treatment. The doctors there had declared in unequivocal terms that

my wife, my daughter and I with Sri Yash and Pam Chopra at a dinner hosted by him at his residence in Mumbai. Also seen is Mr Anupam Kher, a distinguished Bollywood actor.

they could only offer her palliative care but could not assure restoration of mobility of her limbs. Therefore, they came to New York.

I vividly remember her coming to me in a wheelchair. IMRT (Intensity Modulated Radiation Treatment) had very recently made its entry at that time. I started her treatment with that. The treatment went on for 4-6 weeks. In the sixth week, she could stand up. She came walking into my office!

"There is some magic in your hands. Otherwise, this would have not happened," she gratefully extolled me. Her husband, Mr. Yash Chopra, placed a few bundles of hundred-dollar bills on my table. "Whatever, how much soever we pay you, we can't repay your debt. Please accept this and oblige," he pleaded.

I politely refused. I said to him, "I am a full-time doctor here. My hospital adequately compensates me for my duties here. You need not pay anything additionally. Your affection is worth several millions for me."

Shri Yash Chopra was giving us a tour of his Yash Raj Studios in Mumbai sharing with us stories about all the movie awards he received.

Later when I went to Mumbai, he organized a mammoth party for me. A lot of celebrities, including Bollywood actors, directors, and producers attended. Mr. Chopra introduced me to almost everyone and said to them, "He is the doctor who saved my Pam(ela)." I can never forget that evening and the party. Later, he personally took me around and showed me a separate office he had constructed for Yash Raj films and also a big studio. During its inauguration, he threw another huge party and spoke very highly of me, saying, "Because he saved my wife, we remained a complete family and that's how I was able to construct a studio of these proportions." In his office, he made me sit in his chair. His elder son Aditya, daughter-in-law Rani Mukherjee and his second son Uday also show respect for me.

Pamela Chopra came to see the Shirdi temples I have constructed in the U.S. She personally made flower garlands and adorned the deity and had the bells made for Baba's umbrella. She always referred any of her cancer-affected friends and relatives only to me.

Yash Chopra died of dengue. A week before that he spoke to me. I can never forget the affection of that couple. Pam Chopra continued to be cancer free two decades after completing her cancer treatment.

Yash Johar was the husband of Hiroo, sister of Yash Chopra. He was also a big producer from Bollywood. Dharma Productions, which produced many a hit film, was founded solely by him. Karan Johar is the son of Hiroo and Yash Johar.

They were making a movie "Kal Ho Naa Ho," with Rani Mukherjee and Shah Rukh Khan. During its shooting in the New York City, Mr. Yash Johar suddenly fell ill and the tests confirmed that he suffered esophageal cancer.

This news impacted his son Karan Johar and his friend Shah Rukh Khan more than Mr. Yash Johar himself. It was a shock for them. Both were like his brothers. Shah Rukh's father had succumbed to cancer. He used to lament, "Will I also lose my other father to cancer?"

During Yash Johar's treatment with me for 5 weeks in New York, Sharukh Khan came with him to my department every day. I was touched by the deep bond between Shah Rukh Khan and Johar's family, which is very rare in contemporary times.

Keeping aside his sorrow, Yash Johar used to take extraordinary care not to disrupt the shooting. While taking treatment, he used to attend the shooting too. Whenever he was in the hospital both Karan and Shah Rukh would also be at the hospital and spend their time talking to me in my office.

Yash Johar died in 2004 June at the age of 74. A chest infection caused his death. His death very severely impacted both Karan and Hiroo. It saddened them for a long time. Karan, in fact, depicted it in his autobiography, "An Unsuitable Boy". Later, in 2017, Karan became the father of two children, both by surrogacy. He named the boy Yash and the daughter as Roohi, reversing the name of his mother. So much is his love for his parents.*

The sister-in-law of the popular Hindi Hero of patriotic films Mr. Manoj Kumar suffered from cervical cancer. The doctors who had treated her told her that she had completed her treatment and needed only routine check-ups. But the family somehow were not sure and came to the U.S to consult me. After my examination and review of her treatment in India, I informed them that she needed additional treatment. Hence, she continued to complete her treatment under my care, and she was free of cancer for more than two decades.

The wife of a top doctor of AIIMS, Dr. Chaudhary, was herself a leading gynecological oncologist. She had a diagnosis of cancer of the uterus which had spread to the ovaries. She was advised to receive intense chemotherapy. However, she could not endure even the first dose. Doctors could not think of any plausible solution and hence referred her to me. I designed a specialized radiation treatment for her which she was able to complete without any complications. She continues to do well and has been free of cancer for over two decades. She is currently one of the top doctors for gynecological cancers in India. Whenever I am in India, she and her husband meet me and have dinner with me.

The Piramals are a very reputed business family from Mumbai. Mr. Ashok Piramal had advanced kidney cancer when they came to see me in 1984 at MSK. Now, we have the latest target and immunotherapy treatment. But in 1984, we could not help him and eventually he passed away. His younger brother, Mr. Ajay, took over the reins of their business and developed it into a business empire.

Although I could not save Ashok, his younger brother Ajay's wife, Swati Piramal, has been constantly in touch with me, overseeing on-going projects related to cancer, allocating crores of rupees for Prevention/Mitigation of cancer through their family foundation. Her son Anand married Isha Ambani, daughter of Mukesh Ambani.

What is the most notable about all these anecdotes is that the artists, producers, directors, entrepreneurs, celebrities, and many from their families when impacted by cancer have not forgotten what they have gone through. That's why, more often, they stand by and conduct programs to help the affected and donate liberally to the cancer hospitals. Their generosity also inspires others. It is highly commendable.

Shock of cancer diagnosis Letters from my Patients "You have cancer"

While all cancers are potentially fatal, thanks to the enormous advances in our understanding of the natural history of cancer and new and improved methods of treatment, many people who would have died in the past now survive. 40 years after President Richard M. Nixon initiated the "war on cancer" and Congress approved increased funding for cancer research, deaths from all types of cancer have begun to decline.

Indeed, the National Cancer Institute calculates that 9 million Americans who have had an initial bout with cancer are alive today because of intensive research into the causes, diagnosis, and treatment of cancer. In spite of these impressive advances, a diagnosis of cancer is still devastating.

"You have cancer."

"No one is ever prepared to be told that they have cancer," my patient M.C., observed in a letter that she wrote to me about her experience. As a physician who has treated cancer patients for many years, I know she is correct. Cancer is surely the most terrifying medical diagnosis of all. Upon hearing those three words, "You have cancer," or learning that a previously treated cancer has recurred, patients typically experience overwhelming feelings of shock, disbelief, denial, confusion, vulnerability, hopelessness, sadness, and anger. Unless people have been in this situation themselves, it is difficult to understand the depth of feeling and the sense of shock and the resulting feelings of disorientation that such news evokes.

I treated A.G. for prostate cancer in 1991 and his case is typical. He later wrote to me and described his experience.

After my biopsy in 1991, my urologist informed me that I had prostate cancer and that there were three procedures available to me. I could have surgery that might leave me both incontinent and impotent and necessitated an extended stay in the hospital. Or I could have external radiation, involving five weekday visits to the hospital for seven weeks which would likely leave me incontinent and impotent, although to a lesser degree. Or I could have monthly hormone treatments for life with the unappealing side effects of hot flashes and enlarged breasts. My future at this point looked very grim indeed.

Luckily, that same week, my daughter read an article about Dr. Nori who was treating prostate cancer with internal radioactive seeds. At this point I thought I had nothing to lose, and made an appointment.

When the day arrived, Dr. Nori was very patient and frank with me. He described the brachytherapy treatment to me and said that the After effects were minimal, particularly when compared to the other options.

I decided to have brachytherapy and was scheduled for the procedure. Even though the procedure is routinely done on an out patient basis, I stayed in the hospital overnight, because I had come from out-of-state and could be seen by my doctor in case of emergency. In the hospital, I was able to walk around and take care of my personal needs without any assistance from the nurses. My appetite was good and I ate well. The next morning, I was discharged from the hospital and went straight to my office in Paramus, New Jersey. I am an accountant, and since it was tax season, my clients were waiting for their tax returns to be completed. I worked six days a week, ten to twelve hours a day for three months, and then went on a well-earned vacation. As Dr. Nori predicted, I had no incontinence or erectile dysfunction. Upon my recommendations and experience, two of my friends have undergone the same operation and have been grateful to me for telling them about brachytherapy. It's now more than ten years after my brachytherapy and periodic checks show that I am cancer free. I haven't missed a single day of work since my treatment almost two decades ago and the quality of my life couldn't be better. I always thank God that my daughter found that article on Dr. Nori and brachytherapy!

A.G. is just one of thousands of men who are treated for prostate cancer every year. His story is typical of men whom I've treated-he suffered no incontinence, and his erectile function returned in a short time, and he has been coming for regular checkups for the last fifteen years.

R.W. was referred to me in 1993, with a large lump.
I noticed the lump myself on the outside of my left forearm about midway between the wrist and elbow and about three inches

long. I wasn't alarmed and waited a few weeks before deciding to have my doctor look at it. He thought it might be a fatty tissue, which are almost always benign. But just to make sure, he sent me to see a surgeon, who did a biopsy, and it came back positive for sarcoma. He said that he could remove the tumor, but because sarcomas tend to recur in the same site if all the cancer cells aren't removed, he suggested that I have brachytherapy and referred me to Dr. Nori.

When I woke up from the anesthesia, I had several tiny tubes embedded in the spot where the tumor had been. Each day for about a week, Dr. Nori came into my room and inserted the seeds into each tube. Having tubes stuck in your arm for a week certainly looks weird, but except during my treatments, they were covered with a bandage dressing and really weren't uncomfortable. The area was tender for a day or two after the tubes were removed, but that's all.

I went home the day after my last treatment. Dr. Nori said that I should take it easy for a week or so, then gradually resume using my arm normally. Because my tumor was not too extensive, I didn't need physical therapy-my daily household activities served the purpose.

At the time I was diagnosed, I knew next to nothing about cancer and had no idea that sarcoma was one of the most aggressive types. I was also unaware that many people lose their limbs-and even their lives-if treatment isn't done in time. Now that I've learned about how deadly soft tissue sarcomas can be, I feel very lucky to be alive. Surgeons can remove the tumor but it's very difficult to know if they got every cancer cell. Brachytherapy did that. It's been nearly ten years since my surgery. Not only am I alive, but my scar is also almost invisible, and I have full use of my arm!

My patient, K.S., had two tumors in the same breast three years apart.

I found a lump in my left breast in March of 1994. My surgeon did a lumpectomy, removing the tumor and some lymph nodes under my arm. Luckily there were no cancer cells in the nodes. Afterward, I was referred to Dr. Nori and a month or so after the surgery, I started external beam therapy. In the summer of 1997, a second lump was discovered in the same breast during a routine check-up, and it too was malignant. I was advised to undergo mastectomy since yet another tumor might occur, but I refused. So, I had a second lumpectomy in the same breast. Since I had already had an extensive course of external beam radiation, Dr. Nori thought it wasn't advisable that I have any more. Instead, he recommended high dose brachytherapy.

I was hospitalized and had seven treatments-two a day over three and one-half days. At the time of the first treatment Dr. Nori put several needles through the spot where the tumor had been removed, and these remained in place until after the least treatment. They didn't hurt at all, although I was certainly aware that something unusual was there. Each time, Dr. Nori put the high dose seeds in the tubes for about five minutes with the help of a computerized machine called a remote after loader and then removed them. For this, I didn't even need anesthetic. Four days in the hospital isn't a long time, but I didn't feel sick at all and got a little bored being confined to my room. After my last treatment, he removed the tubes, and I was discharged in the afternoon.

My breast was slightly sore for a few days, but that was all. What a surprise, since I had a lot of fatigue during external beam therapy. I returned to my normal routine right away and haven't had any problems for the past 15 years.

Sometimes, tumors of the vagina can recur after years, and without warning. Or a second primary tumor may appear in the same organ. My patient M.B., experienced a vaginal tumor for the second time after being treated for primary cervical cancer.

The thought that cancer invaded my body several decades ago seldom crosses my mind today. Even when it does, it seems as if it all happened to someone I knew, not to me. But if I sit very still and let the emotions return, I can clearly hear a doctor saying that tests showed that I had a second primary carcinoma. How was that possible, I thought. I had convinced myself that having cancer once was like being vaccinated against its return in the future. The physician continued to describe the location and the invasive nature of this second tumor. "You have very few options" he said simply.

What do you mean "very few options," I wondered. I felt great. I was exercising regularly-walking more than twenty-five miles a week. I was on one of my periodic healthy eating regimens. I was successful in my career and happy and content in my personal life. The disease the doctor was describing could not be mine! Surely there was some mistake-an error in identification at the lab. But no. The biopsy slides were mine.

That spring I trudged from one medical specialist to another-each seemed to provide a more dire prognosis than the previous. I endured dozens of tests. After almost two months of searching for options, I found only two of these to be credible. I could do nothing and live for six to twelve months. Or I could have radical surgery and live in fear of periodic infections requiring hospitalization.

I scheduled the extremely radical surgery, knowing that my chances for survival were very slim, and even then I had no assurances that the cancer would be eradicated from my body.

Why me? I had already traveled the cancer route ten years earlier. I was one of a third of the U.S. population who had suffered from some type of cancer, and, I felt, already put in my time, as it were. It wasn't supposed to happen again-not a second primary. I had already had surgery as well as tons of "rads", medical shorthand for "radiation dose".

As I read back over the journals I kept during that period, I am humbled and grateful recognizing how very fortunate I was, after seeing three specialists, to have found yet another who would consider my situation. I met Dr. Nori and was introduced to brachytherapy.

Dr. Nori carefully explained the treatment concept of brachytherapy and outlined the risks in language I could understand. He drew illustrations to explain the procedure he would design for me. He patiently answered my list of written questions but made no promises.

I left that appointment to weigh the risks of brachytherapy versus months of recovery from the radical surgery planned for the following week. If the brachytherapy failed, the radical surgery remained an option, albeit with the possibility of additional complications. According to my analysis, brachytherapy offered me one good year-enough for me to get my life in order. So, I cancelled the surgery and made an appointment for brachytherapy.

My health insurance refused to pay for what was, at the time, still considered experimental, though it would have completely covered the expense for the months of hospitalization anticipated as the result of surgery. I've never been able to understand the rational of this position. Luckily, the out-of-pocket costs for brachytherapy were much lower than for surgery and hospital care. Brachytherapy simply required weekly visits of less than one hour. It was painless. And it left my dignity intact.

Here is the miracle. My second bout with cancer occurred almost twenty years ago. My life expectancy of six to twelve months increased to 20 years. WOW! And still, every single day, I am thankful to be among the thousands of those in the fraternity of cancer survivors, celebrating life.

D.K., one of my patients who had treatment for esophageal cancer describes his experience with diagnosis.

First, I started having difficulty in swallowing. After a few months, it got worse, and I was having extreme difficulty in swallowing anything but liquids. I reported this problem to my primary care physician, and he ordered a barium x-ray of my upper digestive tract. This revealed a blockage in the upper esophageal area and shortly thereafter, an endoscopy exam confirmed my worst nightmare: I had a squamous cell tumor.

The doctors at the hospital told me that the treatment for this esophageal cancer was to have my esophagus removed and that my stomach would be moved up and I would have to be fed through my neck for the rest of my life. They said that they would also remove my voice box so that the margin of tissue around the tumor would be cancer free.

My wife and I were horrified and immediately began exploring other options including non-conventional treatments. A few days after we began searching, she came across an article in the local newspaper quoting Dr. Nori who interviewed about internal radiation treatment for cancer of the esophagus. I called immediately and made an appointment.

Dr. Nori said that he could treat me with intraluminal brachytherapy only if the tumor had not spread beyond the esophagus and did the necessary tests. I was both terrified and hopeful; terrified that I had cancer, and hopeful that it had not spread. My wife, daughter, and I were elated-even joyous-when

Dr. Nori said that it was "contained". With my wife's support and Dr. Nori's agreement, I decided not to have the tumor removed surgically. We would let brachytherapy do the job.

D.K., whose experience with diagnosis is given above, describes his treatment.

My treatment lasted almost two months but was not a disruption to my life. I took my treatment in the morning and went straight to work afterwards. The only side effect I experienced was that sometimes thinking clearly took more effort than it usually did, but it did not interfere with my work, and went away shortly after my treatment was completed. I had no pain or complications and Dr. Nori and the staff were so upbeat, positive and encouraging.

I'm so thankful that my cancer was treatable, and that Dr. Nori encouraged me to believe that I would survive. Once you believe you can survive, you have hope.

D.K. is currently free of cancer 20 years after brachytherapy with no compromise on the quality of his life. David's case is typical for early esophageal cancer. Obviously, treatment, quality of life, and outcome are different for those whose cancers have metastasized. It's very rewarding, however, to see so many of these patients eat again, gain weight, and thrive after treatment, and to know that many of them have significantly longer survival than they would have had in the past.

Louis W. Sullivan, M.D.
President Emeritus
Morehouse School of Medicine
U.S. Secretary of Health and Human Services (1989 – 1993) U.S.A.

Approximately eighteen years ago, in 2000, I was diagnosed with prostate cancer and was referred to Dr. Nori for the treatment. Although I live in Atlanta, I flew to New York regularly over the period of several weeks to receive this therapy under the care and supervision of Dr. Nori, because of his outstanding reputation in medicine and radiation oncology. The outcome was excellent. All signs of prostate cancer were eliminated, and today, some eighteen years later, I remain in good health.

In his clinical care Dr. Nori showed a high degree of skill, professionalism, and compassion with his patients. He also demonstrated excellent administrative and interpersonal skills while managing his clinical and technical staff.

So, I have known Dr. Nori as a fellow physician, medical educator and researcher, and as a former U.S. Secretary of Health, and as a patient treated by him.

Dr. Nori is highly deserving because of his many achievements and contributions to medicine.

I am a former patient of the globally esteemed radiation oncologist, Prof. Dattatreyudu Nori, and I wish to provide a testimony to my life saving experience under his unparalleled professional care over a decade ago (in July 2011). I write also to represent all the global patients who have been helped by the innovative treatment techniques that Dr. Nori developed over the last 35 years at the Memorial Sloan-Kettering Cancer Center and Cornell University.

In 2011, I was diagnosed with prostate cancer, and I consulted several high-level medical specialists across the United States of America, Africa and the United Kingdom. All the specialists referred and directed me to Dr. Nori because of his impeccable scientific credentials and reputation as a world-class pioneering radiation oncologist, with a deep humanitarian spirit.

My experience with Dr. Dattatreyudu was phenomenal. Despite his very busy schedules, he always made time to meet with me, very patiently listened to me, answered all my questions fully, and gave me the very best medical treatment available anywhere. He treated me using the innovative and highly regarded technique of High Dose Rate Brachytherapy which he is widely known to have played an instrumental role in developing.

After my treatment, Dr. Nori met with me several times and explained what the post-treatment prognosis is likely to be, based on his careful analysis of my specific case. I am more than delighted to report that the outcomes have been exactly as he said they would be. I am now fully prostate cancer-free, and my PSA level has fallen well below Zero. It's been nothing short of a miracle. It is not surprising, therefore, that Dr. Nori has received many distinguished awards and honors around the globe.

Finally, I should say that right after my operation, I was so impressed by Dr. Nori's professionalism and humanism that I wrote a special poem dedicated to him.

Dr. Nori merits the highest national honor that your esteemed Government and his beloved native country can bestow on him. He is the best of the best in his field, and a true global leader in the health profession. Dr. Nori exemplifies the Hippocratic Oath in practice to the highest degree, and he is extraordinary in his ability to relate to all across the globe. As an African who has traveled worldwide and interacted with medical professionals on many continents, I can say for certain that Dr. Nori is an exceptional medical scientist and care provider and is a truly inspiring, innovative and exemplary leader in his field.

Yours Sincerely,

Akwasi Aidoo, PhD
Trust Africa
Lot 87, Sacre 3, B.P. 45435
Senegal, West Africa

Closing the Gulf

(for Dr. Nori and Rosalyn), By Akwasi Aidoo The news came

across the Atlantic
breaking the oceanic sounds that drowned
the dreams of trafficked middle passages of centuries old,
flooding the cerebrate with cascading sounds
between disbelief and the why-me angst
Closing the gulf was a bridge to Global City
of melanged India, Philippines, Russia, America and nameless more visages safely spaced behind shrubs of eclectic pieces, V-necked for love Hippocratically Oathed, bouffant-shaped cloth cap, latex gloves
closed toe-shoes to boot my cancer cells to pieces

 The pivot of it all, as I gyrated uncontrollably, were two great souls: Dr. Nori & Rosalyn, anchoring the pellets for the epic battle. His gentle smile caps a global acclaim of perfection
Her unalloyed care bequeaths bouquets of roses.
Together they pulled back my trust of life

Philip Gaitanis

17 Makedonias Street Agia Paraskev, Athens Greece

I live in Athens, Greece and in October 2006, at the age of 54, I was diagnosed with prostate cancer. Terrified, I immediately tried to find the best oncologist here in Greece. They all told me that the best treatment for me was to remove my prostate, that is to undergo surgery. Of the three doctors I visited, right after he saw my test results, prescribed medication, which I found out, was for cancer patients at their final stage of cancer.

In November of 2006, I traveled with my wife to New York. I first went to Memorial Hospital where I saw a surgical oncologist. He told me that I did not need surgery it would be better to see the world- renowned cancer specialist, Dr. Nori.

I saw Dr. Nori at the same time a highly knowledgeable scientist and human being, ready and willing to help his patients in every way. Dr. Nori is a pioneer in these advanced techniques and is considered the father of Brachytherapy in the U.S.A.

Since then I have been to New York to see Dr. Nori for my check- ups. Turning 70 this November 2022, I enjoy life more than ever with my wife, my two daughters, and two lovely grandchildren.

I spend my summers at my country home on a beautiful Greek island. I am still active as a professional engineer, working for a multinational company, and I always think of Dr. Nori, being grateful to him for keeping me alive, for his compassion, his knowledge, his expertise and for an outstanding treatment.

Carlos Sacerdoti
Sacerdoti s.a. Empresa Grafica Mario Bravo 933 Buenos Aires Argentina

My name is Carlos Sacerdoti. I am an Italian Industrial Engineer living in Buenos Aires, Argentina. When I was 61 years old, I was diagnosed with prostate cancer in 2002 and was recommended to contact Dr. Dattatreyudu Nori as he is a pioneer and world-renowned specialist in brachytherapy.

I am grateful to Dr. Nori for his courage, honesty and commitment. I recognize his knowledge not only as a scientist but as a human being ready to act and help patients.

In 2020, I am free of cancer, at present my doctor in Buenos Aires, also a urologist has decided to contact Dr. Dattatreyudu Nori, and plan an exchange training program at his facility in

New York.

M.C. wrote to me about her reaction to being diagnosed with cancer.

"After my examination, my gynecologist chose his words carefully. Nonetheless, I was totally unprepared for what he told me. He said that my biopsy was not benign and there was a tumor on my cervix. I stared at him, unable to think. I knew what the words meant, but my brain refused to comprehend. It was as if I were watching myself in a movie waiting to see what I would do next. Unable to fully accept what I had just heard, my emotions numbed, I watched myself have a rational conversation with the doctor without feeling or really comprehending the meaning of the words. Later I cried a lot, but I didn't feel sorry for myself. I also cried because I had contractions in my uterus every half hour that had me writhing in pain.

M.C.'s oncologist outlined her options.

"He told me that I could have a radical hysterectomy that involved removal of the uterus, ovaries, fallopian tubes, cervix, and upper third of the vagina, or I could see Dr. Nori who did state-of-the-art radiation treatment called 'Brachytherapy.' If I had brachytherapy, I might not need surgery at all. Naturally, I wanted to investigate this option first."

After sitting in the waiting room with other patients, many of whom were ill, M.C. was so nervous that she fainted upon my entrance into the room. All patients are nervous and this is perfectly normal. Fortunately, few pass out from fright. The nurse and I revived her and then we discussed her case. As she recalls:

"After a careful exam, Dr. Nori faced me, looked me directly in the eye, and said simply and directly, 'You have cancer, but there is a cure.' It was the first time a doctor had said the word 'cure' out loud. He went on to tell me that I had a rare form of cancer called adenocarcinoma of the cervix. He told me that the treatment I would have been not experimental -- that it was, in fact, a routine procedure and he was very experienced with it, and that in cases like mine, the cure rate could be in excess of 90%. I liked these odds and suddenly felt more in control!

"I successfully completed my treatment under Dr. Nori and

have been free of cancer for over 37 years."

Nervousness, dread, and even terror, as M.C., the patient who fainted in the examination room experienced, are entirely valid and understandable. In most cases, however, the numbness wears off and "the kaleidoscope of emotions" as one of my patients called it, resolves, at least to a manageable level – enough at least to allow patients to engage in an intensive re-evaluation of their lives and to seek as much information as they can in a very short time.

These patients all went on to have Brachytherapy as their sole treatment or as a boost to external beam radiation. Their letters and many others I've received also contain descriptions of their treatment and recovery, as well as reports of their lives after cancer. These letters have been gratifying for me to read because they offer concrete testimony about the importance of Brachytherapy in cancer treatment.

The significant advantages of my research in Brachytherapy has been very fruitful. When a person is diagnosed with cancer and potentially deadly heart disease, there are sudden feelings of intense isolation and disassociation. At a time when comfort is needed, these feelings can begin a cycle of unfamiliar feelings that can be so overwhelming that it prevents one from taking the steps necessary to carefully evaluate all the treatment options. Many patients have told me that one of the things that helped them overcome the shock of their diagnosis was to find out as much about cancer and their treatment options as they could.

M.A.C., a well-known Puerto Rican journalist and TV personality, was diagnosed with cervical cancer when she was 34 years old. She recalls that her gynecologist, who is a neighbor and friend, came to her house after supper, and gave her and her parents the bad news.

"That night, for me, the world turned upside down. The atmosphere had a strange silence and I felt as if I had fallen into a void. I looked at my parents and my doctor and saw their lips moving, but I could not hear a thing they were saying. What they were saying was that I had cervical cancer, that I must have a hysterectomy.

"Puerto Rico is always warm, but right then I felt so cold. And I will be honest. At that moment, I did not know what hurt more

-- that I had a malignant tumor in my uterus, or that I'd never be able to realize my most cherished dream of having children."

Then she remembers asking "an absurd question": Could the hysterectomy wait for nine months? Her gynecologist told her that the surgery needed to be done as soon as tests revealed whether the cancer had spread. She underwent hysterectomy in her country and unfortunately the cancer recurred when she came to see me.

I treated M.A.C for recurrence after she had a hysterectomy for cervical cancer. After her recovery she wrote to me about her strategy for survival. When I first saw Dr Nori for treatment of my recurrence, I was very dejected, but he and his associates studied my case carefully and explained everything to me. Felt a strong urge to take control and they encouraged me to do so. Together we would work for my healing. The treatment that they recommended there was external beam radiation and Brachytherapy. I was aghast, because it would require me to stay in New York for many weeks, away from my family and fiancé. So, Dr. Nori designed my therapy plan and then it sent to my doctors in Puerto Rico.

Meanwhile, I had found a marvelous book, "Getting Well Again" by Dr. O. Carl Simonton. It gave me the necessary tools to begin my journey on the road to recovery. The first lesson of the book is that we are all participants in our own health. Finding the right doctor is only part of the process. We participate in our health through our beliefs, feelings, emotions, and attitude towards life. How we respond to medical treatment can be influenced by our belief in it and the trust we have in our doctors.

Research has shown that negative emotions produce chemical changes in the body, and Dr. Simonton and other experts on healing argue that positive emotions can produce helpful chemical changes. Love, hope, faith, laughter, and the will to live have therapeutic value. But for most cancer patients this is no easy order. I must admit that there were days when I just could not see the value of this, but as I began to take control of my emotions and concentrated on taking an active role in my treatment, I simply felt better.

I always wanted to know what would be done to me and the

details of how and why. I read every book about cancer I could find, including weighty medical volumes. I memorized my medical records and discussed them with the residents and interns.

Laughter also played an important part in my recuperation. Many people believe that laughter is an infallible remedy, and at my house, we have a healthy dose of it since my mother is a professional comedienne. Although we were not always in the mood for jokes, it was rare that she could not coax a laugh out of us. During my treatment, I began to imitate Dr. Nori's Indian accent (and I am sure that he could do the same with my Puerto-Rican-laced English). One day, I did it for him: "A zimple rectal examinaaazion," I began. He laughed – very hard -- and asked me to do it again whenever I saw him for follow up.

My doctors in Puerto Rico were surprised at my recuperation and asked me what I had done. I told them that I received my treatment from Dr. Nori at MSK Cancer Center. Then they were not surprised as they knew about Dr. Nori and his expertise.

It has been more than 30 years since the day I learned I had cancer. I will always live with that "word" in my mind. Just seeing it in print makes me jump. I will always live with the fear of recurrence, but this fear is overshadowed by what I learned from my encounters with cancer. I learned the meaning of unconditional love from my family, and I learned that "the will to live" is not just a phrase -- it is a reality that can heal.

M. A. C. was a star patient and her multifaceted strategy and assertiveness no doubt played an important role in her recovery.

Over the years, I've had a number of patients from India who were referred to me by doctors I know there. One, S.J.K., came to see me in the early 1980s. S.J.K. used her training as a star athlete to overcome her fears and work with her treatment team. More than 40 years after her treatment she wrote her experiences as follows:

When I was 50 years old my doctor called me at home to give me the results of D & C (dilation and curettage) she had done on me the week before. Casually, as if she were telling me about tomorrow's weather, she told me that I needed a hysterectomy. I took the news casually at first -- both my mother and my sister had had this operation -- so I suggested that I do it after my son's exams were over. "No," she said a bit more urgently. "You have cancer and we should attack it within 24 hours." Suddenly I felt the enormity of the test results: I had been invaded by this scary disease which devastates its victims unmercifully.

Outwardly, the 24 hours passed in an ordered manner. I packed my clothes, did some necessary chores, spoke to my family, but inwardly, I was in turmoil. People and events in my life whirled around in my brain like in a kaleidoscope

I felt that I had let my family down in so many ways and that I could have been a better employee at my job. I felt as if I had been thrown into a huge ocean and had to fight not to go under. I had been a competitive netball (volleyball) player in college, and replayed certain games my team lost in my head. That day, I vowed with all that I held holy, that if I survived and had a second chance, I would fix the things I could fix in my life, and forget about those that I couldn't.

Eventually, the time arrived, and so, on that memorable weekend in December in 1981, instead of attending the wedding day of the child of one of my closest friends, I was wheeled into the operating room to have my uterus removed.

I have no doubt that my participation in competitive sports helped me succeed in surviving cancer. First, it armed me with the will to succeed. My training helped me to focus on a goal (winning), to block out distractions, and to pursue the goal with single-minded passion. My philosophy, developed from years of athletic activity, was, and is: Come what may, I will prevail. Years of competitive sports taught me how to work with a team and this concept helped me enormously when I arrived in New York for my Brachytherapy treatment. I saw myself as a key member of a team and believed that if I did not figure out my part and carry out my part of the game plan, we – I -- might not win.

Many people believe in fate, a tryst with destiny, happenstance. I certainly do. I have read a book. "The Celestine Prophecies" by James Redfield about how incidents in life weave themselves into patterns long before certain events fall into place. My fate, and I believe my salvation was to meet Dr. Nori. He was there, somehow chosen for me and he played a very essential role in my survival for more than three decades now. I was alone with a dreaded disease, in a very imposing hospital, in a strange place. In the first few days, I clung to the idea that I was here for an essential reason, to be treated for this scary disease. Soon, however, Dr. Nori's calm, firm gentleness calmed my fears. At his invitation, I joined the Treatment Team, and together we won a really challenging game.

When I was in New York, alone in my room at night, I vividly remembered the love of my friends at home from India, and frequently their letters and phone calls cheered me up when I was feeling homesick. I used my time alone to think about what I would do with the rest of my life, however long it was. And it has turned out to be long indeed. I was able to take care of my beloved mother for three more years until she died in 1984. I saw both of my sons graduating from college and take advanced degrees. I was alive to attend the wedding of my younger son in 1984. Finally, I was able to care for my husband when he underwent heart by-pass surgery in 1995. There's so much to live for that you just can't contemplate dying…. not for one minute!

Like M.A.C and S.J.K., many patients find that the idea of being a member of a team is both comforting and empowering. It banishes the feeling that you are playing an unfair game all alone and gives you the idea that with the help of your doctor and radiation team, and the love of your family and friends, you can win in a challenging situation.

Z.R.

My patient Z.R., also drew courage and sustenance from friends and turned her time in New York City into a rewarding adventure. She also found that being assertive about her needs to her treatment team made a significant difference in her treatment experience.

Z.R. wrote as follows:

Being a logical person, I asked myself if I wanted to die one day, before I absolutely had to. Of course not! After a long talk with myself, I decided to make the best of the two months I would have to stay in New York City. In fact, I consciously decided to make the best of the rest of my life. My three daughters came to be with me and together we went to the theatre, concerts, and movies. I had several friends in New York, so we made dates with them for dinner in the evenings.

It has been over 34 years since I was treated for my locally advanced gynecological cancer and back then -- it seems like a thousand years ago -- most people were ashamed of having cancer and many kept it a secret even from close friends. For me my friends are a very important part of my life, and I couldn't have gotten the warmth and attention that I received if I had kept my illness from them. I sensed, however, that I had to keep up my part of the bargain. If I was depressed, it would depress them, and no one would have a very good time. So, I decided not to be depressed. Just making the decision made me less depressed. Before going to meet Dr. Nori at MSK Cancer Center in the U.S, I had gotten a second opinion in the U.K and other major cancer centers in the U.S. All the specialists I had met suggested to me to meet Dr. Nori as he had developed cutting-edge and innovative treatment methods for these advanced cancers. The treatment team at the hospital were tremendous and cheered me up at every treatment session. I told them that I didn't like wearing a hospital gown for my treatments. I felt very helpless and began to feel anxious while waiting for my turn on the treatment table. They acknowledged that the radiation works the same whether it's going through a hospital gown or a cotton dress and allowed me to have treatment in my street clothes. This was really a little thing that I could have endured but being assertive about my anxiety and asking for something that was not routine, made me feel so much more in control. Another thing that bothered me was that sometimes I and other patients had to wait what seemed like a long time if there was a delay in the treatment schedule. I told them I made every effort to get to my daily appointments on time, and I felt cheated if I had to wait for a long time. One of the nurses suggested that I call the receptionist and find out if appointments were running on time. If the schedule was delayed, then I could have some additional time to myself. Both minor alterations in the normal routine were enormously helpful to me.

After two months of external beam treatment and Brachytherapy, I returned home to continue my normal life. I paid special attention to my appearance because, I surmised, everyone expected to see a corpse. But in many respects, life after treatment was not "normal." I appreciated life more than ever before and took nothing for granted. Every beautiful sunset, every moonlit night, every trip I took, every party I went to - gave me ten times more pleasure. Today when there is a family gathering or birthday, I am so grateful to God, to medical science, and to Doctor Nori for the wonderful present he gave me -- life. In the past 34 years, I've seen three of my four children get married and have been blessed with two gorgeous granddaughters. I became chairman of an investment company that provides fascinating work for me.

I hope that my experience provides encouragement to others who are going through a similar experience. If you are as frightened and surprised as I was, don't feel alone. If you thought, "How could this happen to me?" others have been there. if you are bewildered and overwhelmed by so much medical information that seems written in a foreign language, take heart. Do your research as quickly and efficiently as you can...... Make sure that you are at the best hospital you can find

for your problem and take the time to find the best doctor to do the job, like Dr Nori. Then, trust your doctor to do the best job possible and become an active member of your treatment team. There is life after treatment, it may be for you, as it was for me, the sweetest part. You cannot believe how wonderful life feels. We are married now 60 years and 33 of it is due to the miracle of your work.

With my Patient Z.R. from Israel During my visit to Jerusalem

N.B.

I treated N.B. for recurrence of vaginal melanoma in 1986 and again in 1996. As she remembers:

"I was stunned, numb - incapable of even asking questions. I wished I had let someone go with me to my appointment, but I had rejected this idea as childish. I was an intelligent and independent adult, I thought, and asked myself why I would need anyone to go to the doctor with me?"

Initially, her doctor recommended radical surgery to remove not only the tumor, but her uterus and most of her vagina, rectum, and bladder as well!

"During that very long weekend after my diagnosis, it was a question of whether to accept what I saw as mutilation or do nothing and die of the melanoma.

I was sixty-one, not all that thrilled with my life, and I wondered why I should put myself through such a drastic operation -- and its aftermath. How one functioned with practically nothing left below the waist, along with incontinence, possible digestive problems, and no sexual feeling defied contemplation. On the other hand, how was it going to be to die of cancer? That too defied contemplation."

After further tests, N.B.'s oncologist told her that her condition was not quite as cut and dry at he had originally believed, and he referred her to me for an assessment.

"I shall never forget that meeting. At the conclusion, Dr. Nori said, 'Since this would be radical surgery, I could try radiation - if you agree.' If I agreed? So, I had six weekly treatments of Brachytherapy on an outpatient basis, and at the end, the melanoma was gone. No nausea. No mutilation. It would be an understatement to say that I was extremely grateful."

She was free of cancer for more than a decade after the treatment.

All the above-mentioned individuals continue to be hale and healthy and free from cancer today.

Conclusion

After a century of experimentation, innovation, and refinement, radiation therapy has fulfilled its initial promise to save or prolong many lives that would otherwise be lost to cancer. But healing and survival often require more than technology. They take confidence, more than a little determination, hope, and the will to live -- as long and as well as possible.

Chapter 23
PROVIDENT PERSPECTIVE OF A PROFESSIONAL: MY OBSERVATIONS AND MY SUGGESTIONS ABOUT CANCER CARE IN INDIA"

Part I

Significant milestones

1. Indian Council of Medical Research established a National Cancer registry in 1981.

2. With initial support from Tata Memorial Trust, the National Cancer Grid was established in 2012 with 56 member institutions, and with membership increasing to 250 in 2021.

3. In 2018, India established the National Cancer Institute on par with the National Cancer Institute of the US.

4. From 2015 to 2020, the scope of cancer services at all the regional cancer centers has been expanded with subsidized cancer care by various governmental programs, and an extensive media campaign on the lethal effects of tobacco was undertaken.

A few organizations forewarned of the impending burden of cancer in India. Yes, this is true. We shall be ready. The collated data suggests that India is in a take-off stage regarding the treatment of cancer. A few good initiatives have been launched. We may have to add a few more.

As we are getting better at controlling and treating all communicable diseases such as TB, smallpox and others, the impact of NCD (Non communicable diseases) is becoming a major issue for all the private and governmental organizations in developing countries. Cancer is at the top of the list in this epidemiological transition. Unless we develop innovative strategies to prevent or mitigate cancer through health education, to detect cancer with precision screening techniques, and to treat it with advanced techniques, we are heading towards increasing incidences of and deaths from cancer.

In India, currently about 1300 to 1500 people are dying every day due to cancer, and over 200 to 300 women are dying daily due to cervical cancer.

As my mentor, Dr. Kottmeier, Head of the International Cancer Organization (FIGO) in Stockholm once observed, cancer deaths of female heads of household have a great impact on the long-term sustainability of families.

In India, we witnessed an alarming increase in breast and cervical cancer occurrences over the past decade. More troubling is the age at which women are developing these cancers: younger women from 35 to 45 years old.

There are regional variations in cancer incidence in India because of environmental, socioeconomic, and lifestyle factors. All of these are in addition to genetic predispositions to the disease.

For example, esophageal cancer is more rampant in the North- Eastern states of India due to excessive tobacco consumption.

In West Bengal, the lung and bladder cancers are more prevalent.

In the South and the coastal areas, the spicy food habits induce more stomach cancers caused by Helicobacter pylori (H. Pylori). In Goa, colon cancer is the result of red meat and alcohol consumption.

As they chew tobacco and pan masala, the people of Gujarat are affected more by head and neck and mouth cancers. In Punjab, all kinds of cancers such as kidney, urinary bladder, and breast cancers are found because of the toxic residues of pesticides and other chemicals that are sprayed on the agricultural fields and crops. In the Ganges belt, Uttar Pradesh, Bihar, and West Bengal, because of the toxic remnants of the river, gallbladder and head and neck cancers are more prevalent.

In Madhya Pradesh mouth-cancer numbers are high due to consumption of tobacco and pan masala. In fact, 60 to 70% of the cancers in India are caused by tobacco consumption.

Part II

Based on my extensive experience in oncology, spanning

about 50 years, during which period I have helped various governmental and academic cancer programs around the globe, I would like to suggest the following for consideration for India:

1. The leadership of our newly established NCI are doing great work in streamlining the oncology-related activities in the country. In my view, NCI should be given more administrative authority and resources to be the main center of operations for all oncology-related activities in India. It should begin implementing new programs at an accelerated pace as we have had a late start. In addition to providing state of the art clinical care and research, just like at the US NCI, our NCI in India should have independent departments or divisions, organized as follows:

- Population sciences and cancer control Cancer mitigation and prevention
- Precision diagnostics and precision treatment Training and research strategy
- Oversight of RCCs (regional cancer centers)
- Cancer centers accreditation (voluntary or mandatory) of all cancer programs in the country
- Grants and research funding Reduction of health disparities
- Task forces development and strategic plans for highly prevalent cancers e.g., breast and cervical cancers
- Pain and palliative care programs

I am certain that some of these departments are already in place. If not, they should be established at the earliest date.

2. In India, there is already an existing infrastructure with partially or fully funded RCCs (regional cancer centers), medical college oncology programs, and district hospitals. Our NCI should take advantage of these incredible resources to implement its programs.

3. The prevalence and the mortality from cancer of the breast and cervix are increasing at an alarming rate. There is an urgent need to establish a high-level task force under the NCI to

streamline programs for health education, precision screening and precision treatment at clinical sites.

4. Our NCI should invest resources to strengthen our local, regional, and national cancer registries and make cancer diagnosis a reportable disease, as it is in the US.

5. Our NCI should establish a nationwide toll free "cancer hotline" number so that patients from anywhere in the country can get information regarding their treatment at an approved cancer program in their region.

6. Tobacco consumption in the US has gone down significantly over the past decade. Under the auspices of our NCI, India should enhance anti-tobacco campaigns in all schools, colleges, and universities.

7. Cancer care should become accessible and affordable. Subsidized care plans from both central and state governments should be enhanced significantly. The charges for cancer diagnosis and treatment from all cancer programs in the country should be made available on the internet, preferably with treatment outcome data from various programs.

8. Programs for pain and palliative care should be highlighted at all the regional cancer centers under the auspices of the NCI. In addition, the ICMR and IMA should develop post graduate courses at all medical colleges in the country in this important domain of pain and palliative care specialties.

9. About 80 to 90% of cancers in children are currently treatable and curable. Our NCI should explore the opportunities to establish 4 to 6 pediatric cancer centers with public and private partnerships, like the St. Jude's Children's Hospital in the U.S. (While there is a Department of Pediatric Oncology in Kidwai Institute of Oncology, Bangalore, it might be inadequate at the present time.) Cancer care for children should be offered free of charge.

We have a significant shortage of oncologists in India. We will not be able to catch up with the need unless we develop innovative programs. Qualified M.D graduates should be provided with a crash course, a six month's course in oncology and then should be able to treat patients with standard protocols, and for complicated cases, they should be the liaison physicians to refer the cases to regional cancer centers.

All the above suggestions can be brought under the umbrella of "Ayushman Bharat," an initiative by the current government of India. Once these measures are implemented, their mammoth impact will manifest soon, and the incidence of cancer can be considerably reduced. If cancer is detected early, many lives can be saved; many families can survive; their finances can be safeguarded. Both as an expert doctor of the domain as well as a simple person of humanitarian values, this is what I wish to see happening.

Advances in understanding of cancer that are changing the treatment paradigm

What are the new advances like?

The difference between earlier treatments and these new advances such as Molecular Twin (MT), Next-Generation Sequencing (NGS), immunotherapy, and precision medicine tools we use today is like the difference between a simple back-up camera in your car and a 360-degree surround-view camera.

Let us look at some of them.

"Molecular Twin" (Cedar Sinai) is a scientific stunt double who is always in the lab ready to test out new theories and perhaps reveal important details of how cancer is affecting your body. Molecular twin is an innovative tool to help diagnose and precisely treat cancer through the convergence of multiple biological physical and computational technologies.

The causes of cancer are a combination of genetic, environmental exposure and random mutations. These causes manifest themselves in the landscape of a tumor, the changes that take place in the cells as they progress from normal to cancerous such as somatic mutations or epigenetic modifications.

The future of cancer treatment and cure will come from better understanding of this vast landscape. Several unaddressed questions will get answered with this knowledge such as

How do biomarkers for cancer change over time and in response to treatment?

Do markers differ by race and ethnicity?

Can some new markers replace the need for imaging and

invasive diagnostic technologies?

NGS

Next-Generation Sequencing (NGS) is a new technology used for DNA and RNA sequencing and variant/mutation detection. NGS can sequence hundreds or thousands of genes or a whole genome in a short period of time. The sequence variants/mutations detected by NGS have been widely used for cancer diagnosis, prognosis, therapeutic decision, and follow up of patients. The capacity of its massive parallel sequencing offers new opportunities for personalized precision medicine.

Necessity of NGS technology

One of the advantages of NGS is to interrogate many targets at the same time on the scale of hundreds and thousands or even millions of targets. Such capacity gives NGS huge potential application in clinical settings. For example, in cancer patient care, any given tumor may have multiple mutations. If the traditional molecular assays are used in such clinical settings, multiple assays may have to be performed for multiple mutations. A larger tissue sample may be needed for these multiple assays. Using NSG technology, these targets can be interrogated in one test. Therefore, less tissue is needed and the results of dozens and hundreds of DNA targets are obtained from one test.

In a patient's sample, the leukemic cells bearing the same mutations are believed to originate from the one clone. A patient's sample with many mutations may have more than one clone of leukemic cells. A leukemic disease may not only have more than one clone of leukemic cells, and the clones may change during the course of the disease. Such a phenomenon is referred to as clonal evolution. A similar phenomenon has been observed in solid tumors too. This observation has changed the old one tumor-one mutation concept. A solid tumor may have multiple mutations. These mutations can originate from one clone or multiple clones. This is called tumor mutation heterogeneity. Therefore, in cancer patient care, multiple gene mutations have to be tested very often. Due to clonal evolution many different gene mutations need to be tested during follow-up. Besides, not only solid tumors may have multiple mutations, but metastatic tumors may also have mutations different from that of the primary tumor. Such findings also indicate that multiple mutations need to be tested by diagnostic and follow-up molecular tests. With the advent of immunotherapy, tumor mutation burden has become an important parameter to be tested. This again needs to investigate numerous mutations in a tumor sample. A higher mutational burden in the tumor means a higher response with immunotherapy. The traditional molecular test methods are not useful for such needs. Therefore, NGS technology becomes necessary for such tasks in patient care. Moreover, in the current medical practice, although biopsy samples become smaller and smaller, more information related to mutation need to be extracted from small biopsy samples. In many cases, it is impossible for the traditional molecular tests to meet such needs. NGS has evolved to meet such needs. By massive parallel sequencing, NGS technology can test multiple samples and multiple targets at the same time. Therefore, it increases the turnaround time of the molecular tests. It has become clear that NGS technology is an important tool in personalized precision medicine.

Immunotherapy

As the tumor grows in the body, it dismantles the molecular shield. It makes our body lose grip on our immunological system, which is the command-and-control system of the body.

The mechanism that underlies cancer immunotherapy differs considerably from those other approaches to cancer treatment. Unlike chemotherapy or targeted therapy, cancer immunotherapy relies on an anticancer response that is dynamic and not limited to targeting a single oncogenic derangement.

Cancer immunotherapy can therefore lead to anti-tumor activity that simultaneously targets many of the abnormalities (targets) that differentiates cancer cells and tumors from normal cells and tissues. In summary this newer class of agents that work by stimulating the immune system and not directly by killing cancer cells. Immunotherapy is a game changer in the management of many cancers.

Chapter 24
Artificial Intelligence (AI) and Cancer

AI presents an unprecedented opportunity to advance our understanding of cancer and improve care for people with cancer. Artificial intelligence (AI) is a machine's ability to perform functions that are usually thought of as intelligent human behaviors, such as learning, reasoning, and solving problems. Computers derive this ability from algorithms that enable the use of data to make predictions or to create new content. AI algorithms can detect patterns in large amounts of data that cannot be easily perceived by the human brain. In recent years, advances in three areas—methods and algorithms for training AI models, computer hardware needed to train these models, and access to large volumes of cancer data such as imaging, genomics, and clinical data—have converged, leading to promising new applications of AI in cancer research.

These new applications include understanding and predicting biological mechanisms, finding and leveraging patterns in clinical data to improve patient outcomes, and disentangling complex epidemiological, behavioral, and real-world data. Implemented in an ethical and scientifically rigorous manner, these uses of AI have the potential to rapidly advance cancer research and create better health outcomes for all. In 2024, the Nobel Prize in Physics was awarded to John Hopfield, PhD, and Geoffrey Hinton, PhD, for their pioneering work in artificial neutral networks, which laid the foundation for modern AI applications in cancer research. Their contributions have sparked a revolution in the field, with machine learning now driving advances in diagnostics, drug discovery, and precision oncology, profoundly reshaping cancer research and care.

AI's biggest leap in oncology so far has been in diagnostics, more specifically in radiology, where advanced image analytics are transforming how we detect and diagnose cancer. "AI can now analyze scans faster and with greater accuracy, helping doctors catch cancer earlier. AI's capacity to analyze enormous datasets, including patient genetics, clinical history, and tumor profiles, could allow for highly personalized treatment plans tailored to individual patients. This holds the potential to move beyond traditional, one-size-fits-all treatment methods.

The future in oncology lies where AI meets biology. We are on the cusp of using biocomputing to process biological signals directly, which could allow us to make real-time treatment decisions based on live data from the patient's body. That's a game-changer. The next wave of innovation will come from integrating AI with biological systems, pushing us into an era where medicine becomes even more personalized, precise and predictive.

We are living in a transformative era for cancer research, the overall death rate is declining steadily, and the number of cancer survivors has reached an unprecedented level. This remarkable progress is driven by breakthroughs across all areas of cancer science and medicine, even tackling once intractable diseases such as advanced lung cancer and metastatic melanoma. Fueled by trailblazing scientific discoveries and technological innovations, we are now positioned to achieve even greater advances that will save countless more lives.

Artificial intelligence-based approaches are beginning to transform cancer detection, diagnosis, treatment decision making and response monitoring.

Chapter 25

THE WAY FORWARD

Today cancer is a common household word with each of us closely associated with at least one near or dear one, a family member, a friend, a relative, or a colleague diagnosed with cancer. In India there is also a perception that the incidence of cancer is on the increase and with a hope that perhaps with the advances in technology and cancer being diagnosed at an early stage, the myths associated with cancer are vanish "Pap" testing" and mammography have contributed to more than 70% decrease in cervical cancer mortality since 1969 and a 42% decline in breast cancer mortality since 1989. According to the American Cancer Society 2022 reports, a substantial proportion of cancers could be pre- vented including all cancers caused by tobacco use and other unhealthy behaviors. At least 45% of newly diagnosed cancers in the U.S., about 805,600 cases are potentially avoidable. The same is true in India.

Globocan estimates that by 2025, there will be a substantial increase in cancer cases from 12.3 million to 19.3 million cases. Fifty percent of these will be in developing countries, with India contributing to 8 to 10% of the cases. The Globocan focus on combating cancer needs to be on "cancer awareness," early detection, diagnosis, and availability and affordability of treatment in all cancers.

The amazing aspect of the human genome is the minimal variation in DNA sequence in the genome of different individuals. Of the 3.2 billion bases, roughly 99.9% are identical between two individuals.

It is the remaining tiny fraction of the genome 0.1% that makes a person unique. This small amount of genetic variation determines key attributes which determine the individual's chances of developing cancer and their response to treatment. One's chances of getting cancer are affected by the lifestyle choices made.

Simple lifestyle changes can make a profound difference:

1. Listen to your body for any unusual signs and symptoms: any lumps, persistent cough, fever, swelling, irregular bowel habits, bleeding, etc. Do not ignore them and seek medical attention.

2. Inquire about your family history with cancer and take appropriate early diagnostic interventions if there is a strong history of breast, ovary, endometrial, or prostate cancer.

3. Tobacco consumption in any form can initiate and promote cancer. Also, alcohol consumption, and consumption of fried and preserved foods.

    Tobacco consumption can cause lung, mouth, throat, laryngeal, pancreatic, bladder, cervical, and kidney cancers.

4. Eat a healthy diet

    To reduce the risk of developing cancer

a) Eat plenty of fruits, vegetables, and greens.

b) Avoid obesity.

c) Consume alcohol in moderation to minimize the risk of breast, colon, lung, kidney, and liver cancers.

d) Limit processed foods.

5) Maintain a healthy weight and be physically active. Doing so lowers the risk of breast, prostate, lung, colon, and kidney cancers. Activities can be as simple as a thirty-minute walk each day.

6) Protect yourself from excessive exposure to sunlight.

7) Get vaccinated for Hepatitis B to prevent liver cancer and with the HPV vaccine to prevent cervical cancer.

8) Avoid risky behavior in all activities of life; also practice safe sex

9) Get regular medical check-ups; perform self-examination; and get regular follow-up screening for breast, prostate, lung, liver, and colon.

10. Avoid exposure to environmental toxins such as pesticides,

herbicides and other chemicals. Take appropriate safety precautions while using them such as wearing gloves and face masks, etc.

The fear of cancer can be overcome only by knowledge.
It is in the journey of discovery, invention and innovation in cancer treatment that we conquer new frontiers of knowledge and come to know new solutions.
As the Sanskrit adage goes

"Nahi jnanena sadrusham" –
"Knowledge has no parallel"

FAMILY

Names of my brothers, sisters and their spouses:

Sisters	**Brothers-in-law**
Padmavathi Pillalamarri	Sambasiva sharma
Anantha Lakshmi Nimmagadda	Krishnamoorthy
Seetha Mahalakshmi	Picchaiah Meduri
Maha Tripura Sundari Burra	Ramalinga Sastry
Indira Devi Sastry Lanka	Satyanarayana
Rama Devi Sharma Lanka	Madhusudana

Brothers	**Sisters-in-law**
Radhakrishna Murthy Nori	Satya vani (Guntur)
Mrutyunjaya Rao Nori	Kanakadurga
(Addepalli) Venkata Ramamohan Rao Nori	Srilakshmi
(Jonnalagadda) Madhura Babu Nori	Madhavi (Burra)
Ramatheertha Nori (Panchagnula)	Suguna

Myself	**My spouse**
Dattatreyudu Nori (Tadepalli)	Subhadra

My children	**Their spouses**
Sateesh Nori (Son)	Joy Kanwar
Priya Nori (Daughter)	Himanshu Nagar

Grandchildren

Prana Maheswari Nagar , Abhinaya Nagar
Shaan Kumar Nori, Jhansi Estella Nori

Messages of Support

N.V. Ramana
Chief Justice of India
New Delhi-110 001

Supreme court of India
Tilak Marg,

English Translation of video message
in Telugu given online by Mr. Justice Nuthalapati Venkata Ramana,
Hon'ble the Chief Justice of India at the launch of "Odigina Kalam".

MESSAGE

Dr. Nori is a standing testimony to humanity embodied.

By presenting his life of seven decades with full of service and achievements in the form of this book titled "Odigina Kalam" Dr. Nori rendered great service to the society, particularly the Telugu society.

This book is one of the Books that I had completed reading in one go. This book not only spreads the message of the popular adage "Service to the mankind is service to God" but also is a treasure trove of knowledge. While reading the hardships he faced in his childhood, the sacrifices of his mother, the affection of his family, the support lent by his near and dear, my eyes welled up. This real-life story touches everyone's heart.

Although he was constrained to join B.Sc. initially, he proved to be a winner with his undaunted focus to pursue his favorite subject of medicine. He displayed the same dedication in rendering service to the society - whether by building the temples of medical treatment for the needy or building the temples for the devotees of Sai in the U.S. It enabled him to cross several milestones in life moving ahead as an extraordinary leader by taking along one and all in his mission.

In this book, he describes medical science and cancer in very simple language. Adding the testimonials of several patients who vividly described their experiences really made this book more interesting. Though many incidents in his life just seem to be purely coincidental, his extraordinary achievements in serving the humanity at large are as per the divine will. Dr. Frank Ellis' visit to Hyderabad, Dr. Nori coming in contact with him, Dr. Ellis' invitation to him to visit the U.S. later, Dr. Nori's entry into one of the most renowned cancer research centers of international repute with his support; his fortune to serve several cancer patients across the world, his coming in contact with influential persons, through them extending the modern technology and medical facilities to several countries etc. ... reading all this, one is sure to wonder if it was an illusion or reality. In this book, there is a message for developing countries -like ours-too. He has elucidated in this book about the relentless research that is going on in the U.S. Even our country has to gear up to that level. The statistical data also has to be collated. The facilities and the infrastructure to match what Dr. Nori could obtain in the U.S. shall be provided in our country too to equip the experts.

    He laments that he could not afford to admit his own father-in-law for treatment in the institution where he was working. Although initially the AIIMS of Delhi came to his rescue, the later medical compulsions for modern treatment for his father-in-law at the U.S. drove his finances haywire. If indigenous research can be fortified and such modern facilities could be provided within our country, such treatment can become affordable to everyone.

    I am surprised to learn that as far back as five decades ago, Dr. Nori used computer technology in Brachytherapy. Both such modern technology and his caliber are required for our country to strengthen its infrastructure of medical care. This invaluable autobiography should inspire our young scientists, doctors and policy makers. Our country should adequately utilize his knowledge and services. In Chapter10 of this book, what Mr. N.T. Rama Rao (NTR), the then Chief Minister of Andhra Pradesh spoke about D. Nori was aptly quoted:

"There are many a capable doctor like Dr. Nori who are willing to redeem their debt to their mother land. We shall utilize their services. I might be a hero for Telugus, but Dr. Nori who has been toiling in the field of medicine and relentlessly fighting against deadly cancer is the "Real Hero".

What NTR said was the absolute truth.

There is no discrimination in the U.S. -avers Dr. Nori. Whichever country Dr. Nori visits, he wouldn't find any discrimination as the world is one's reflection. His pleasant demeanor and gentle talk are always reciprocated everywhere. Not only his talk is sweet, but his professional caliber is equally excellent. Dr. Nori's empire of medical excellence is as sprawling as the erstwhile British Empire where Sun never set. In every nook and corner of the world, one can find his patients who could get a second life after being brilliantly treated by him. Although, he reached the zenith of his career, he never forgot his roots. By bringing up his children with same Telugu traditions and legacy, he has set an example for other Telugus of the diaspora.

Such a fine human being and gentleman also could not escape some unsavory experiences in life. In Chapter 13, he describes- with anguish- one such episode and about his resilience to come out unscathed after almost two years of enquiry - nothing short of the saga of mythical Sita of Ramayana who went through the ordeal of fire. Having seen such lowest ebbs myself, I can certainly understand his pain and distress. Truth prevails.

The six guidelines he suggested to both commoners and the Doctors in Chapter 23 & 24, would go a long way in safeguarding one's health. Similarly, his advice to hospitals and the Government and to all of us are worth following. I have also requested him several times to help my friends, relatives and colleagues. I am greatly indebted to him for saving the lives of many of them.

We are fortunate that he hailed from our land. I earnestly wish that he will continue to serve the mankind and save many more lives.

I heartily congratulate his wife Dr. Subhadra, who solidly stood by him at all times, and their children. I also congratulate Dr. Nori for giving us such beautiful book and also Mrs. Aruna Pappu for collaborating with him in the endeavor and its publishers 'Sahitee Mitrulu'.

Best Wishes,

Nuthalapati Venkata Raman

February 2022

TO THE READER,

As one of the many, many patients from around the globe who are alive today because of our Dr. Nori, I was delighted to read his autobiography. I was fascinated to read about the man, his life story, his values, his many achievements, and his dreams.

Back in 1984 when he treated me for a rare form of cancer, he was already a highly respected radiation oncologist at Memorial Sloan- Kettering and then went on to hold simultaneous top leadership positions at New York-Presbyterian, Cornell and the Arnold Center at New York Hospital Queens. However, the book gave me a new view of our Dr. Nori as a little boy who lost his father at the age of six, who grew up in poverty in India, who was nurtured by a selfless mother and huge supportive family. Told with sincerity, warmth, humor, and humility, the book shows the story of his youth and his struggles to get his education and medical degree, and those who helped him along the way. It tells of his coming to Manhattan with only his M.D and $15 in his pocket to land the job at MSK, his many Gurus, his family, his patients, his hard work, his advances in Brachytherapy, his setbacks and triumphs as he gradually became a world-respected authority in his field. The book also describes his initiatives in transforming a small hospital in Queens, New York to a major cancer center, and in making state-of-the-art cancer treatment accessible to the poor in India, while it tells of those who helped finance and realize these endeavors. The book also details his efforts to train doctors to disseminate his expertise world- wide.

There's glamor too, as I read about the once poor little boy, now a famous doctor, hanging out with celebrities and the rich and the famous who were his patients, and who both inspired Dr. Nori and were inspired by hm to service and philanthropy.

It was also illuminating for me to read that this man of science is so deeply spiritual. His reverence for his religious beliefs and Indian culture shows another dimension of Dr. Nori.

More than autobiography, the book also gives important information about recent and current developments in cancer treatment. And in more personal terms, it presents the stories of cancer survivors, offering hope and encouragement to patients newly diagnosed with cancer, as well as to their families and friends – and their doctors.

In fact, overall, this is a book about hope.

Marie Czarnecki
Czarnecki
Utica, New York, USA

ACKNOWLEDGEMENTS

New York-Presbyterian Queens

Natalie Masino
Office Manager
Department of Radiation Oncology

Fred McCready Administrative Director Department of Radiation Oncology

Adrian D. Osian
Director of Physics
Department of Radiation Oncology

Vijaya Malladi
Cancer Center Manager

Dr. George F. Heinrich
Chairman, Board of Trustees

Stephen S. Mills
President and
Chief Executive Officer

Arthur Dawson, Ph.D.
Chairman
Board of Trustees

Ned R. Arnold
Life Trustee

Dr. Herbert C. Rader
Chief Medical Officer

New York-Presbyterian/Weill Cornell Medicine

Dr. David B. Skinner
President and Chief Executive Officer

Dr. Thomas A. Caputo
Professor of Obstetrics and Gynecology

Dr. Mark W. Pasmantier
Clinical Professor of Medicine, Hematology Oncology

Dr. Parul Shukla
Director of Postgraduate Education Professor of Surgery

Memorial Sloan-Kettering Cancer Center

Dr. Edward J. Beattie
Chief Medical Officer

Dr. Samuel Hellman
Physician-in-Chief

Dr. Zvi Fuks
Chairman, Department of Radiation Oncology

Dr. Florence Chu
Chairman
Department of Radiation Oncology

Dr. Basil S. Hilaris
Chief, Brachytherapy Service Department of Radiation Oncology

Lowell L. Anderson, Ph.D.
Chief of Medical Physics

Dr. Manjit S. Bains Min H. and Yu-Fan C. Kao Chair in Thoracic Cancer

Dr. Jatin P. Shah
Elliot W. Strong Chair in Head and Neck Cancer

Dr. Nael Martini Chief of Thoracic Service Department of Surgery

Dr. Frank Ellis
Chairman Emeritus
Department of Radiation Oncology

About the Author

Dr. Dattatreyudu Nori is an internationally acclaimed oncologist, par excellence, a pioneering physician, and an important thought leader. During his career spanning over four decades, he has held the positions of Chief of Brachytherapy at Memorial Sloan Kettering Cancer Center and Professor and Chairman of Oncology and Director of the Cancer Center at the world-renowned Cornell Medical Center in New York. He has pioneered numerous cancer treatment techniques that have contributed to significant improvement in the cure rates and in saving lives of countless cancer patients all over the world. He has also taken special interest in making sure that these advances reached vulnerable and poor cancer patients in developing countries. He has written over 300 scientific articles and four books in oncology and trained over 300 residents and fellows who are now occupying leadership positions around the globe.

Dr. Nori has extended his expertise and experience to various governments and private organizations to establish comprehensive Cancer Centers. In early 2000, he helped the government of Andhra Pradesh and was one of the founding members and Chief Scientific Advisor of the Basavatarakum Indo-American Cancer and Research Institute in Hyderabad, a 750 bed not for profit, Comprehensive Cancer Center.

He is also a consultant to the United Nations International Atomic Energy Agency (IAEA), advising in the formulation of guidelines for cancer treatment in developing countries. His distinguished and exceptional achievements in the field of oncology have been recognized with many fellowships, awards, and honors. He received the most prestigious "Tribute to Life" Award presented by the American Cancer He is recognized as one of the Top Doctors for Cancer in the U.S. and Top Doctor for Women's Cancer in the U.S. for over three decades by his peers of 100,000 oncologists.

The government of India recognized his contributions to medicine with the "Padma Shri" Award in 2015, one of the highest civilian awards.

He is also honored with the highest civilian award in the US "The Ellis Island Medal of Honor" for his exemplary and outstanding qualities in both his personal and professional life. In 2017, the 10,000 member oncologists of the Indian Cancer Congress honored him with their highest recognition "Living Legend in Cancer" award for his contributions to cancer care in India, the U.S. and around the globe.

Currently, he is Senior Advisor to Memorial Sloan Kettering Cancer center -i-cliniq-India operations.

Society and the "Most Distinguished Physician Award" presented by Memorial Sloan-Kettering Cancer Center. The American Association of Physicians of Indian origin (AAPI) honored with the "Most Distinguished Physician Award".

He is recognized as one of the Top Doctors for Cancer in the U.S. and Top Doctor for Women's Cancer in the U.S. for over three decades by his peers of 100,000 oncologists. The government of India recognized his contributions to medicine with the "Padma Shri" Award in 2015, one of the highest civilian awards.

He is also honored with the highest civilian award in the US "The Ellis Island Medal of Honor" for his exemplary and outstanding qualities in both his personal and professional life. In 2017, the 10,000 member oncologists of the Indian Cancer Congress honored him with their highest recognition "Living Legend in Cancer" award for his contributions to cancer care in India, the U.S. and around the globe.

Currently, he is Senior Advisor to Memorial Sloan Kettering Cancer center -i-cliniq-India operations.

THANK YOU

With a deep sense of gratitude and appreciation, I would like to thank the contributions of my teachers at my primary school, high school and college, medical school and university for invaluable guidance. From J. Branch School, Jai Hind High School in Masulipatnam, Majeti Guravaieh High School in Guntur, B Camp High School in Kurnool, Kurnool Medical College and Hospital, Gandhi Hospital in Secunderabad, Osmania Medical College and Osmania University in Hyderabad. Without their help and support and imparting great education and values in me, I would not have become who I am today. My sincere thanks to all of them.

I am also grateful and indebted to my professors from Andhra, Sri Venkatweswara and Osmania Universities, especially Dr. D.P. Bhaskar Reddy, Dr. P.S.R.K. Haranath, Dr. P.V. Chalapathi Rao, Dr. V. Krishna Mohan, Dr. Abdul Qureshi, Dr. Varanasi S. Subbarao, and Dr. Aswani Kumar.

I want to extend my special personal thanks to all my oncology colleagues in India who helped in the treatment of my patients in India. Dr. P. Jaganath, Dr. P. Desai, Dr. Asha Kapadia, Dr. Ramesh Sarin, Dr. S. Hukku, Dr. G.K. Rath, Dr. T. Subrahmanyeswra Rao, Dr. P.S. Chandrasekhar, Dr. M. Babaiah, Dr. T. Vijayanand Reddy, Dr. C.H. Mohan Vamsey, Dr. P. Dattatreya, Dr. Krishna Ragu and Dr. R. Senthil.

I am grateful and thankful to all trustee members of Basavatarakam Indo-American Cancer Institute, especially former Secretary Sri K. Krishanam Raju, former Chairman (late) Dr. K. Siva Prasad and current Chairman Sri N. Bala Krishna, CEO Dr. R.V. Prabhakara Rao, and Director fo Education Dr. Kalpana Raghunath.

I sincerely thank and convey my best wishes to my family members who followed me in my profession as a Dr., Dr. M. Lakshmi Sarada, Dr. M. Srinivas, Dr. Nori Priya, Dr. Himanshu Nagar, Dr. C. Bindu, Dr. Nori Vijaya Bhaskar, Dr. Nori Kameswari, Dr. Lanka Nityanand and Dr. Lanka Annapurna. Most important, my special thanks to Mr. R. Pratap Reddy for his excellent translation of my Telugu autobiography book and to Marie Czarnecki for her editorial review.

My special heartfelt thanks to Natalie Masino, for the revisions in the text and compilation of chapters in this book and my utmost sincere thanks to my brother Sri Nori Ramatheertha for his continuous guidance in completing the Telugu and English books of my autobiography.

I need to make a particular special mention of my gratitude to the news and electronic media in our States of Andhra Pradesh and Telangana. More particularly about Eenadu group. They made it possible for me to propagate and educate and enlighten our Telugu people all about cancer and my contributions and achievements. I want to convey my humble and sincere respects to Sri Ramojee Rao garu.

Dattatreyudu Nori, M.D.

A meaningful photo of my life journey.
Having had begun life with meagre resources,
to become a world-renowned oncologist was a dream come true.

This picture is in a private jet on my travel from New York to New Delhi to see a patient.

Additional Photos

With NY Governor Kathy Hochul

With Neera Tanden
Chairperson for Domestic Affairs,
at White House receiving my book for the White House Library

With Chief Minister of Andhra Pradesh
Shri N Chandrababu Naidu

With Indian Ambassador in
New York City on India's Independence Day

In Times Square NY, Honored by
Senator Schumer, Kathy Hochul,
Governor of New York, and
Eric Adams, Mayor of New York City

At the White House.

With George Walker Bush, president of the United States

with U.S. President Barack Obama

the U.S. Senator Hillary Clinton

With Vice president of India in New Delhi attending an international oncology meeting at All India Institute of Medical sciences

Receiving tribute to life award from Dr Rader, American Cancer Society.

Receiving the most distinguished physician award from AAPI (American Association of Physicians of Indian origin) in Chicago for my contributions to oncology in the U.S. and India.

"The most distinguished physician-scientist" award from the Memorial Sloan-Kettering Cancer Center in New York.

Lifetime achievement award given at the British parliament U.K. by Sanskriti foundation.

a living legend in oncology
award from the Indian Cancer Congress in 2017.

Receiving Dr.Y. Nayudamma Memorial Award

Receiving very prestigious
'Fellow of American College of Radiology' recognition

Mr. Shivraj chief minister of Madhya Pradesh honoring me at the Lincoln Center in New York during his visit to the U.S.

With my colleagues from Memorial Sloan Kettering cancer center at the residence of Prime Minister of India Smt Indira Gandhi in New Delhi. This International oncology meeting was organized by me.